PELVIC POWER!

The pelvic girdle—formed by the hip-bones and lower spine—contains some of the organs most vital to a woman's health, and the related muscles are equally important.

"The benefits of pelvic exercise go far beyond the prevention of medical problems. Not only can exercise improve your appearance and the way you feel, but strong pelvic muscles are essential to a good sex life."

—Kathryn Lance and Maria Agardy

This book was written by women, for women of all ages, and contains exercises for the pelvic area that are easy to do and which take as little as five minutes a day to perform—a boon to every woman.

SEXUAL
HEALTH
AND
FITNESS
FOR
WOMEN

KATHRYN LANCE AND MARIA AGARDY

CORGI BOOKS
A DIVISION OF TRANSWORLD PUBLISHERS LTD

SEXUAL HEALTH AND FITNESS FOR WOMEN

A CORGI BOOK 0 552 99011 6

First publication in Great Britain

PRINTING HISTORY

Corgi edition published 1983

Copyright © 1981 by Kathryn Lance and Maria Agardy

This book is set in 10pt. Times Roman

Corgi Books are published by Transworld Publishers Ltd.,
Century House, 61–63 Uxbridge Road,
Ealing, London W5 5SA

Made and printed in Great Britain by the
Guernsey Press Co. Ltd., Guernsey, Channel Islands.

Acknowledgments

This book could not have been written without the generous help of a number of people. Although we do not have room to mention them all, the following were especially helpful.

We would like to thank first of all our gynaecological consultant, Dr. Peter Liebert, who took the time from his very busy schedule to review the manuscript for medical accuracy. His suggestions and support, as well as his good humour, have been invaluable.

For further help with technical questions, we'd like to thank Dr. John Myers, Dr. J. B. Skelton, and Dr. Satty Keswani.

No book can be completed without the patience and support of friends. We would especially like to mention the following: Joann Rasmussen, Robbin Reynolds, Diane Greenfield, Dolores Querques, and Mark Salmon. Thanks also to Eleanor Rawson for the time and care she has given to the manuscript, and very special thanks to Ray Siegener, who brought us together.

Finally, we want to thank all the women who have faithfully performed the exercises and been willing to talk about their own experiences in the hope of helping other women to achieve pelvic fitness.

Contents

Foreword

By Peter B. Liebert, M.D.
Department of OB-GYN at Mount Sinai Hospital

In the last decade women have effectively begun to regain control of their bodies in a multitude of ways. One of the most significant of these has been the dissemination of sound gynecological information, bypassing the sombre filtration of the medical establishment. The landmark in this area was *Our Bodies, Ourselves*.

Sexual Health and Fitness for Women coming a decade later, is surely in that same mould—by women about women for women.

Kathryn Lance and Maria Agardy have effectively described a series of steps that many women will be able to adopt to counter some of the adverse effects on their pelvic structures that may occur with child-bearing and aging. They deal with a number of general benefits and several specific conditions in which these exercises can be valuable, and have articulated a conception of self-determination for women's sexual and reproductive well-being.

This book is very much a product of this era and probably could not have been done before now.

Part One

Feminine
Fitness

What This Book Can Do for You

by

Kathryn Lance

This is a different kind of exercise book.

For one thing, it was written by women and for women. The exercises in it are easy, and they take as little as five minutes a day to perform.

Second, and most important, the exercises are exclusively for women. The basic routine wouldn't do a man any good.

The fact is, this is the only exercise book that tells you about the ways in which your fitness needs are different from a man's, and shows you how to fill those needs. This is not information that you will get in other exercise books, in the average co-ed exercise class, or even in most fitness classes geared to women.

Yet the exercises presented in this book are essential for the continuing health and fitness of women of *all* ages. Whether you are a teenager who has just started having her periods, a young mother with two small children, or a grandmother well past menopause, the programmes in this book can help you to look better, feel better, and regain or maintain health in one of the most important areas of your body: the pelvic area, which cradles the organs that make you, a woman, unique. As a bonus, these exercises are *guaranteed* to improve your sex life.

Before I go on, let me tell you who we are and how this book came to be written.

Maria Agardy, who looks ten years younger than her age, grew up in Hungary, where she routinely participated in exercise and sports from early childhood. As a teenager, she was physically daring, even piloting aeroplanes. However, as a young woman she became very ill with a disease that damaged her liver, and by the time she came to

15

this country with her husband and young daughter, had resigned herself to a life of semi-invalidism.

One day a friend of hers, who knew of Maria's background in physical fitness, persuaded her to fill in and teach an exercise class for a few weeks. Soon Maria was teaching several classes a week on a regular basis. As she continued to devote more time to exercise, she noticed that gradually all of her physical problems began to disappear. Today Maria radiates vibrant good health.

As a result of her own experiences, Maria decided to devote her life to teaching other women how to maintain wellness through physical fitness. In the last eighteen years she has spent more than 12,000 hours teaching exercise classes. Maria's classes, which are offered in several New Jersey towns, are usually crowded—both with women who have been with her for years and with new students, who have heard about the miracles she produces.

'Maria's classes are different,' says Joan, a twenty-seven-year-old teacher. 'You can tell she really cares. Since I've been doing her exercises I get compliments on my body all the time.'

'Maria changed my life,' adds another woman. 'After my divorce I was overweight, flabby, and depressed. I started going to her classes every night just to cheer up. The next thing I knew I was thinner, my waist was slim again, and I had control of my life.'

A forty-two-year-old mother of three sums up the effect the classes have had on her and others: 'I love Maria,' she says. 'She's inspirational.'

What makes Maria's exercise classes so special? Apart from her warmth and concern for her students, Maria is one of very few exercise instructors who recognize that a woman's exercise needs are different. Although her routines include well-balanced exercises to improve the strength and flexibility of the entire body, Maria concentrates on that area of the body that is most important to a woman's special fitness needs: the muscles surrounding the pelvis.

It was while teaching a class to women who had difficulty conceiving children that Maria became aware how widespread poor pelvic fitness is among otherwise healthy American women. 'American women are very weak in the pelvic area,' she maintains. 'They do not move freely. Many of them have such a poor condition of the pelvic floor that they suffer needlessly from a poor sex life. Some conditions caused by weak pelvic muscles can even lead to surgery if they continue to be neglected.'

16

I am one of the women whom Maria is talking about. My early experiences were the exact opposite of Maria's. As a child and a young woman who became a full-time free-lance writer, I was so sedentary as to be practically immobile. Except for necessary short walks, I got virtually no exercise until eight years ago, when I developed high blood pressure. This scared me into activity, and I began a programme of vigorous exercise which not only helped solve my health problems but gave me a trim figure and an appreciation of the importance of physical fitness for the rest of my life.

When Maria and I were introduced by a friend, Maria told me about the importance of pelvic fitness. This was news to me even though I had been reading and writing about exercise for nearly a decade.

Maria asked me to take a simple test (which we present in a later chapter), and I confidently agreed, certain I would do well: after all, I run ten miles a week, I lift weights, and I have been doing so for nearly eight years.

I failed the test.

I was shocked and upset with myself until Maria explained that *no matter how much or what sort of exercise you are now doing, the muscles of the pelvic floor cannot be strengthened unless they are exercised directly.* Furthermore, she told me, many women have been using these muscles incorrectly since childhood, which prevents them from becoming strong and healthy.

Unable to resist a physical challenge, I began to perform the exercises Maria recommended. They were so easy to do I wondered if they were working; in any case, since I was fit and had never had children, I remained sceptical that they would do anything for me.

I couldn't have been more wrong. After a few weeks of exercise, I noticed that something was different, in a subtle way. I had more feeling in my pelvic area, and an awareness of the pelvic floor that I had never before experienced. When I went for my next routine Pap smear, my gynaecologist confirmed that something had, indeed, changed: my vaginal muscles had become so much stronger that I required a new diaphragm size!

Now, in itself, this may not sound like a dramatic result (although my gynaecologist was quite impressed); however, it gave me tangible proof of how greatly I had neglected the health of a vital part of my body. Moreover, as I began to attend Maria's exercise classes and learn more about pelvic fitness, I saw how lucky I was that the poor condition of my pelvic muscles had not yet caused any definite health problems.

One young mother, for example, had been suffering for years from an embarrassing involuntary leakage of urine whenever she engaged in any strenuous activity. 'It got so bad I was almost afraid to leave the house,' she says. Her doctor had diagnosed the problem as a very weak bladder wall, caused by child bearing, and told her that the only cure for the condition was surgery. After six months of doing the exercises recommended by Maria, this woman returned to her doctor, who 'was thoroughly amazed. "The muscles are tight and firm again," he said. "What have you been doing?" When I told him I'd been exercising, he said, "Oh, no, exercise never works." But I have proof that it does.' This same woman reports that her husband, too, has noticed the benefits of her exercise programme. 'For years sex had been more of a routine than a pleasure for us,' she says. 'But now my husband says I'm getting better as I'm getting older.'

An improved sex life was a common side effect for women of all ages. Miriam, a housewife in her late twenties, credits Maria with saving her marriage. 'I was a mess when I started her class,' Miriam says. 'I was overweight and had no self-confidence. I thought my husband had lost interest in me. Maria put me on a diet and told me about the pelvic exercises. After just a few weeks my confidence came back. Because of the exercises I knew I was a better lover, and my husband and I became closer than ever. He says I'm like a new woman now.'

Other women echoed Miriam's praise, telling of how pelvic fitness led to fewer premenstrual and menstrual troubles, and easier pregnancies and deliveries. A young woman who had recently delivered her third child in as many years says, 'The exercises are a miracle. After my second child I thought my figure was gone forever. But I started exercising when I got pregnant with the last baby. The day after the birth I began again, slowly, and in just a few weeks my body was as slim and firm as it was when I was a teenager.'

Many of Maria's students are women who had not exercised in many years. Without exception they spoke with gratitude of feeling better and seeing minor health problems disappear. Their enthusiasm is exemplified by Sally, who has been in Maria's classes for six years, and who has enrolled her daughter. 'I wish there were some way for all women to know about these exercises,' she says. 'They are one of the most important things a woman can do for herself.'

Pelvic exercises are so important, in fact, that Maria believes they should be taught routinely to young girls in grade school.

Until that utopian time comes, however, any woman, no matter what her age or how out of shape she is, can begin doing exercises for pelvic fitness and start to see the results in a very few weeks. Some of the benefits will be immediate and dramatic, while others will become apparent with the passing years. They include:

• for young women, reduced premenstrual and menstrual distress and pain;

• for women of childbearing age, a more comfortable pregnancy, an easier labour, and quicker recovery after delivery;

• for middle-aged and older women, fewer of the problems sometimes thought to be inevitable with advancing years, such as a sagging abdomen, decreased vaginal tone and sensitivity, and that distressing, embarrassing involuntary leakage of urine;

• *for women of ALL ages, a more pleasurable sex life*.

Pelvic fitness is not difficult to achieve—all it requires is doing the exercises on a regular basis for several weeks until minimal fitness is attained. Maintaining that fitness is even easier, taking as little time as twenty minutes a week!

The exercises require no special equipment or expertise, and because they are divided into easy, intermediate, and advanced, any woman can do them, beginning from any level of fitness. There are additional, optional exercises for special conditions, such as back pain and pregnancy, and special times of life, such as first menstruation and menopause.

Although there is information in this book that your gynaecologist probably never told you, it is not our intention to compete with or conflict with medical advice. Rather, we hope to make you more informed about and more the mistress of your own body, so that you can truly be a partner in the care and health of the organs and muscles of your own female pelvic area.

If you have never before stuck to an exercise programme, this book represents a unique opportunity for you. It is for you and for all women. It is nothing less than a lifelong guide to feminine fitness, and it is our hope that you will use it to improve your health, appearance, and well-being as a woman.

2

Feminine Fitness:
A Woman's Special Needs

It's not news that women and men are built differently; you have only to look to see that this is so. We are softer, rounder, and have wider hips, while men are larger, more muscular, and streamlined. The most profound difference between us, though, and the one that is most obvious but seldom mentioned in discussion of fitness, is that we are designed to carry and deliver the future members of our race, while men are not.

The physical stresses of childbearing are well known to most women, through reading or personal experience. What is not so well known is that these strains can be minimized and their ill effects prevented or reversed by proper exercise. Furthermore, *even women who do not plan to have children can benefit from proper training of the muscles most important in pregnancy and birth*.

Unfortunately, very few women are aware of the importance—or in some cases of the very existence—of these muscles. Even women who have done pelvic exercises during and after pregnancy are seldom taught that the condition of these muscles is important from earliest childhood onward.

This is so for a number of reasons. Traditionally, and even given the current interest in sports for women, few women of any age are accustomed to thinking of exercise as a preventive or cure for anything, and certainly not in conjunction with the health of the internal organs. As Margie, a young dress designer, puts it, 'Sure I exercise—for about two months a year, right before bikini season.'

Not only do many of us believe, with Margie, that exercise has only cosmetic effects, there is also a widespread feeling that we must not be concerned or even curious about our own bodies. It is true that this Victorian attitude is beginning to change, largely due to the women's health movement and to such excellent books as *Our Bodies, Ourselves,* and *The Ms. Guide to a Woman's Health.* Still, the benefits of pelvic exercises are usually taught only in classes for pregnant women; those who do not have access to such classes remain largely unaware of the many benefits to be gained from pelvic exercises. Furthermore, for most women, the most serious problems caused by weak pelvic muscles do not appear for some years. And when such problems do arise, no matter at what age, the afflicted woman is not likely to be told that exercise can relieve and in some cases cure the condition.

'But That's Normal at Your Age'

Tania M., a young mother of four, found herself becoming increasingly tired, with backaches and an aching feeling of 'heaviness' in her pelvic area. Though she wasn't overweight, her waist and abdomen sagged, and, as she put it, 'I was barely thirty, but I felt and looked middle-aged.'

Tania's family doctor prescribed tranquillizers and advised her to get out more. 'I'd like to see him get out more with four small children,' Tania observes. A second doctor acknowledged that her problems were in part physical, but added, 'What do you expect after four children?'

'He told me my problems were normal,' Tania reports. 'But I couldn't accept that. I remembered some exercises I'd learned in my natural childbirth classes. I thought it couldn't hurt to start doing them. It's hard to find time to exercise every day, and I'm still not 100 per cent, but the difference is amazing. I'm beginning to find out what normal really means.'

Tania's instincts are right. It is *not* normal to suffer any condition that can be eased or corrected (or, more to the point, prevented) by using your muscles the way they were meant to be used. Healthy, properly worked muscles do not sag and let go. Your body, after all, was made to last a lifetime. And this is as true for the muscles surrounding your pelvic area as for any muscles in your body.

Furthermore, the benefits of pelvic exercise go far beyond the prevention of medical problems. Not only can exercise improve your appearance and the way you feel, strong pelvic muscles are essential to a good sex life. From the time of Freud onward there has been a

22

persistent myth that unresolved psychological conflicts are responsible for women's frigidity or inability to have orgasms. In a large number of these cases the cause is simply poor muscular tone and incorrect use of the pelvic muscles. Countless hours and tens of thousands of dollars spent on an analyst may help you to greater self-understanding, but they will not strengthen the muscles that are important for proper sexual functioning. *In a questionnaire filled out by members of Maria's exercise classes, 'more feeling during sex' and 'more frequent orgasms' were among the most common benefits of these exercises listed by women of all ages.*

Incredibly, the amount of time that must be devoted to exercising the pelvic muscles is less than five minutes a day. The exercises can be done anywhere, and are so easy that any woman—no matter how busy or out of shape—can begin right now to retrain these muscles and improve her health, appearance, and well-being. Some of them can even be done invisibly when you are out in public, at work, waiting in line, or travelling to a destination!

Women's Fitness and the 'Experts'

None of this should be startling news, but for many women it will be. It is almost as if there has been a conspiracy of silence to keep women from realizing their birthright to a healthy, fully functioning body. The conspiracy, of course, is no such thing: it is rather the result of that tradition of female inactivity we mentioned earlier and a reluctance on the part of fitness experts and doctors to address, specifically, the needs of women.

Unfortunately, we as women have aided in this 'conspiracy' by abdicating responsibility for knowledge of and control over our own bodies, particularly the parts of our bodies concerned with reproduction. Even with the growth of feminism and the natural childbirth movement, many women are still unprepared for the physical demands of sexual development, pregnancy, childbirth, and the inevitable changes of menopause. In *For Her Own Good*, Deirdre English and Barbara Ehrenreich point out that from the early days of medicine there has been a trend to let the 'experts' take control, to listen to their counsel rather than to the wisdom of our own bodies.

The problem with this approach is that the experts have mostly been men, and as men, they simply have not thought in terms of a woman's needs. Furthermore, again because of men's domination of the fitness and health fields, there has been surprisingly little research done into a woman's actual need for physical activity.

Until very recently, for example, it was taken for granted that a pregnant woman should remain as inactive as possible throughout her pregnancy. The old stereotype of the nervous young husband who insisted on doing everything for his pregnant wife only reflected the prevailing belief that any exercise could be harmful to the prospective mother and child. Yet studies are beginning to show that just the opposite is the case. In fact, it is now known that a woman who *maintains* a regular, vigorous exercise programme throughout her pregnancy is more likely to have not only an easy labour and delivery, with fewer complications and need for drug intervention, but also a quicker and more complete recovery afterwards. Today it is not uncommon for women to continue to jog or engage in other exercise through the ninth month. (It is still true, however, that pregnancy is not the time to *begin* a strenuous exercise programme.)

Likewise, women with menstrual cramps have traditionally been excused from any taxing activity, even though there is now evidence that *exercise is one of the best cures for this condition*.

In short, it has been in the area of specifically *feminine* fitness, the fitness of the pelvic muscles and organs, that women's need for exercise has been most widely ignored. The traditional point of view has been that pelvic strength is not only unnecessary, it's not even worth considering. And nowhere has this attitude been more widespread than in the field of gynaecological medicine.

Unnecessary Operations

'My grandmother had one, my mother and my aunts had one, and I always assumed that when I got to be forty I'd have to have one too.' The above quote is from a young woman in her early thirties who is active in the women's health movement. What she is referring to is a hysterectomy, which today is one of the most frequently prescribed operations in this country. Recent studies have shown that this traumatic operation may be performed unnecessarily more often than any other major procedure. Hysterectomies have in the past been recommended for everything from menstrual cramps to lack of sexual desire, and even as a prophylactic measure to prevent a woman who is through bearing children from someday, possibly, developing uterine cancer!

24

Another gynaecological operation which is frequently, and often unnecessarily, performed is surgery to correct a 'loose' vagina, to improve urinary control and lovemaking for women whose pelvic muscles have been damaged by childbirth. Yet this very surgery may make intercourse painful for the woman and merely tightens, rather than strengthening the weak muscles involved.

We don't mean to imply here that our nation's gynaecological surgeons are a pack of bloodthirsty butchers, but the fact is that a surgeon is trained in surgical procedures and will naturally look to surgery for the answer to many conditions that might be corrected by other, less drastic means. Furthermore, even those doctors who are well aware of the value of exercise may reason that their patients are not motivated enough to devote the time and practice necessary for results from exercise. Even the excellent book *It's Your Body: A Woman's Guide to Gynaecology*, which states that 'surgery should be considered the last resort in the treatment of any condition, except in emergency situations,' devotes practically no space to exercise as a preventive or treatment for many of the ailments that are peculiar to women.

Sadly, this attitude continues despite abundant evidence indicating that many conditions that are now routinely corrected by surgery can be prevented and even cured by pelvic exercises.

One of the most common and dramatic examples of these conditions is urinary stress incontinence, which afflicts many women from the thirties on, particularly those who have borne several children. The primary cause of this condition, in which even sneezing or laughing can result in embarrassing involuntary leakage of urine, is a weak or damaged pelvic floor muscle. While it is well known that any muscle responds to exercise by becoming stronger, exercises to correct or prevent urinary stress incontinence are seldom prescribed. Rather, the afflicted woman is told simply to put up with it or is operated on. This common resort to surgery continues despite the fact that the exercises were first prescribed and tested by the respected gynaecologist Arnold Kegel in the 1950s.

In a later section we will explain other conditions that may be treated or prevented by exercise, and show you how to avoid them or relieve the symptoms.

After all, our bodies were made to bear babies, and there's no reason why this perfectly natural function should be debilitating. But sadly, thousands upon thousands of women continue to suffer needlessly from illness and a less than optimal sex life because they have not been informed of the simple steps they could take to strengthen and improve the health of their pelvic muscles.

All of this is not to say that exercise is a cure-all for everything. Certainly for many disorders surgical or other medical intervention is the best treatment. But you will respond best to any treatment if your body is already fit. And in any case, if you begin a programme of regular exercise for pelvic fitness, you will not only become stronger and healthier, you will feel and look better.

The exercises in this book do not promise you total fitness. Pelvic exercises are not a substitute for a complete exercise programme using all the muscles of your body, and we will have more to say about this in a later chapter. But pelvic fitness is vital to a woman's well-being throughout her life, whether she has children or not, and the advantage of the exercises presented in this book is that they are so easy and take so little time that any woman, no matter how out of shape or how busy, can perform them and begin to reap their benefits in as little as six weeks' time.

3

The Most Important
Muscles in a Woman's Body

A young woman we know indulged in a lifelong fantasy and gave herself belly dancing lessons for her thirtieth birthday. After her first few lessons she reported, discouraged, 'I thought all there would be to it was wiggling your hips a little. I never realized there were so many muscles involved!'

The muscles that are used in belly dancing, as a matter of fact, are those we have been talking about: the muscles that surround the pelvis. The health of the entire pelvic area—inside and out—is largely dependent on the condition of those muscles. Because the pelvis is involved in so many functions, ranging from posture and balance to the health of the internal organs, these muscles are among the most important in your body. *Poor condition of the pelvic muscles can cause stress which may manifest itself in other parts of the body, such as the head and the neck*. Pain in the feet and legs, for example, is sometimes the result of sciatica, or irritation of the sciatic nerve, which is the largest nerve in your body and travels through an opening in the pelvis all the way down your legs. In fact, since a number of nerves and blood vessels pass through openings and notches in the pelvis, any condition in which the pelvis is not aligned correctly can lead to pinching or irritating these nerves and vessels. Thus, a pelvis distorted by muscular stress or imbalance can not only cause pain, it may even contribute to circulatory problems in the lower body, including haemorrhoids and varicose veins.

That so many of us suffer from these and other disorders is evidence that the pelvic muscles are simply not in good shape in most women. In fact, inactivity and flab have a lot of us in such poor shape that we're tempted to give up. The good news, however, is that all of these muscles respond quickly and readily to exercise.

Furthermore, there are only three major muscle groups you need to work on to improve your own pelvic fitness.

The Abdominals

'I've dieted till my arms look like matchsticks. And I still have to wear a girdle if I don't want my stomach to stick out!'

If this sounds familiar, you are not alone. Unless you are obese, the culprit in that protruding abdomen is not overeating so much as it is weak abdominal muscles. *More than any other muscles in your body, the condition of the abdominals is most apparent.* Weak abdominals show—in a sagging stomach, a concave back, and 'middle-aged spread' (which can begin in the twenties!). Although a protruding stomach can be temporarily controlled with a girdle, or hidden by loose, shapeless clothes, only exercise will correct the underlying poor condition. This does *not* mean that you have to train yourself to do 100 sit-ups and leg lifts every morning; what is necessary, however, is enough moderate exercise, such as the exercises in our programme, to tighten and strengthen muscles that function very much like a natural girdle.

There are actually several muscles included in the abdominal group. The central muscles run from the bottom of the rib cage to the pubic bone. The main function of these muscles is to curl the trunk forward (which is why sit-ups strengthen them). They also support the contents of the abdominal cavity. The side abdominal muscles are set slantwise like the inset panels in a girdle, and their main function is to twist the trunk and to bend it to the side. (These are the muscles that are most important for a slim waist and firm midriff.)

Unfortunately, most women, particularly if they have been inactive or have borne children, have very poor abdominal muscle tone. The first sign of weakness is usually a protruding abdomen. Since one of the major functions of the abdominals is to hold the contents of the abdominal cavity in place, weak muscles allow the organs to sag against the abdominal wall. The result: it literally 'all hangs out.'

All the abdominal muscles help to keep your trunk upright and aid in maintaining good posture, which helps prevent fatigue as well as improving appearance. If you doubt this, remember the last time you took a look at yourself in a full-length mirror, especially from the side. The chances are you automatically sucked in your abdomen for

28

the *look* of a five-pound weight loss. Strong abdominal muscles will help you keep that look all the time—not just when you consciously think about it.

Backache, too, can be caused by weak abdominal muscles. In fact, many experts believe that the most important cause of backache in most cases is an imbalance between the muscles of the abdomen and those of the lower back. That is, the abdominal muscles, no matter how strong, are weaker, relatively, than the back muscles. The resulting imbalance pulls the spine and pelvic area out of alignment, resulting in pain. According to Dr. Hans Kraus, a noted back specialist, in most cases the abdominal muscles of persons with chronic back conditions are less than one-third as strong as their back muscles. This may seem surprising, because few of us consciously do exercises for the strength of our backs, but the fact is that our lower backs (and the muscles in the backs of the legs) receive exercise in the mere process of walking, while the abdominal muscles do not.

Strong abdominal muscles can also help to prevent constipation by squeezing the contents of the abdominal cavity. Because of their importance in posture and control of the upper body, they are essential in all sports, and of course they work with the uterus during the process of childbirth, in pushing the baby down the birth canal. While strong abdominal muscles will not guarantee total health of the abdominal area, if you should ever need abdominal surgery, your recovery will be much quicker if the muscles are strong to begin with.

The Lower Back

'In two years I've gone from a size eight skirt to a ten,' says Penny, who works in an insurance office. 'But I'm still a size eight on top. And I haven't gained an ounce. What's going on?'

What's going on with Penny, as with the majority of women who hold office jobs, is too much sitting. Just as flabby abdominal muscles mean a protruding stomach, a weak lower back means hip spread and a sagging derriere. Improper sitting, improper diet, and recent childbirth can make this condition worse. (A great deal of sitting, as a matter of fact, is bad for anybody, and if your work requires you to sit for hours at a time, it's important to try to take an activity break every hour or so.)

The muscles of your lower back are responsible for straightening your trunk. They work in opposition to your abdominal muscles, which curl the trunk forward. They also work with your abdominals in maintaining good posture and in all activities in which your trunk must be stabilized, such as carrying, lifting, and all sports.

Although the lower back muscles are, as we explained earlier, usually stronger than the abdominals, this does not mean that most women have strong, healthy lower back muscles. On the contrary, if your abdominal muscles are out of shape your lower back muscles are likely to be out of shape as well. In other words, although your back muscles may be stronger than your abdominals, this strength is only relative, and exercises to strengthen and stretch the lower back are every bit as important to the fitness of the pelvic area as are exercises for the stomach.

No matter how strong your lower back muscles are, the chances are that they are tighter and less flexible than they should be. A too-tight lower back can lead to poor posture and stiffness, and can aggravate the problems associated with weak abdominal muscles.

The exercises in our programme will help you build strength and flexibility in this important area. As a bonus, the flexibility exercises feel good and can be used to relax and refresh your whole body.

The P-C: the Least Discussed Muscle in Your Body

And now we come to what is probably the third most important muscle in a woman's body, after the heart and abdominals. This muscle is not directly connected to your stomach, thighs, or back. Unlike all the other muscles in your body, it is not helped by sit-ups, by stretching exercises, by daily living, or by most sports. The only way this muscle can be exercised, in fact, is by direct exercises designed specifically for that purpose. Yet it is seldom even mentioned in fitness books and programmes, and chances are that unless you've been given pre- or post-pregnancy exercises to do for it, you haven't even heard of it.

This very important muscle is sometimes called the pelvic floor. Its technical name is the pubococcygeus, or P-C for short.

To understand why the P-C should be virtually unknown to most of us, as well as why it is so vital to your health, let's take a closer look at the pelvis itself.

The 'Magic' Bowl

The word *pelvis* comes from the Latin word for basin, and as you can see in the drawing, it is indeed shaped very much like a bowl, with a generous amount of room inside. The most obvious function of this bony bowl is to hold and protect the contents of your abdominal cavity, but the pelvis is vital to the functioning of your body in many other ways as well. Surprisingly, for example, no fewer than fifty-seven muscles are connected to the pelvis. These include muscles that help to move your arms as well as the more obvious abdominal, back, and leg muscles.

The pelvis also serves as a shock absorber in movement, preventing jolts that occur when you walk, run, or change position from being directly transmitted to the vertebrae, the chain of tiny bones that forms your spine. The pelvis is thus involved in all movement, and affects your posture and therefore appearance in all positions.

If you are not overweight you can actually feel part of your own pelvis where the bony parts are near the surface. To do this, stand comfortably in front of a mirror, wearing loose clothes. The easiest

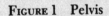

FIGURE 1　Pelvis

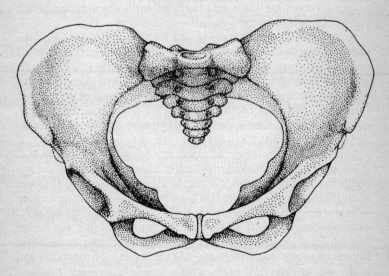

part of the pelvis to locate is the front part, called the pubis, or 'pubic bone.' This is the hard bone you feel just underneath your pubic hair. A couple of inches higher and to the sides are the two projections of your hip bones, which represent the front-most part of your upper pelvis. By pressing gently and firmly you can follow that ridge up and behind part way to your back. The back of the pelvis, called the sacrum, can be felt as a hard flat area above your buttocks, ending in the tiny coccyx, or 'tailbone,' between your buttocks.

Although the pelvis is made up of several bones which are fused together, the resulting structure is not completely rigid. In fact, there are three joints within your pelvis, each of which allows some small degree of movement. Thus, this bony bowl is not only strong enough to help support a growing baby through nine months of its mother's daily activities, it is adaptable enough to allow the mother's posture and centre of gravity to change, adjusting to what can amount to a considerable gain in weight, and is also flexible enough to allow the baby to pass out of its mother's body when the pregnancy is at term.

This final remarkable capability of the pelvis is possible because only the sides of the pelvic bowl are bony. The *bottom* of the pelvic bowl is a flexible, stretchable muscle: the P-C.

You can think of the P-C as a kind of cone-shaped hammock, suspended from the sides and backs of the bottom of the pelvic bones, descending to the area between your legs.

As you can see in the drawing, the P-C is a very thin, sheet-like muscle composed of several parts, each having extensions. For all practical purposes, it behaves as one muscle because all of the parts are interconnected; while they have separate functions, one part of the P-C cannot move without the others becoming involved to some extent. In addition to providing a floor for your abdominal cavity, this very complex muscle also controls your urine flow, the contractions of your vagina, and your anal sphincter.

Considering all its important functions, it is surprising that the P-C is not a thick band of muscle like many other major muscles in your body, but there is a reason it is not. In lower animals the P-C serves many of the same functions as it does in humans, including closing off the open end of the pelvic bowl. (It also helps to move the tail.) The important difference is that animals for the most part walk on all four legs, and so the actual 'floor' of the pelvis is at the back, while the muscles responsible for supporting the contents of the abdominal cavity against gravity are the much stronger abdominal muscles. When humans began walking upright, the result was that the

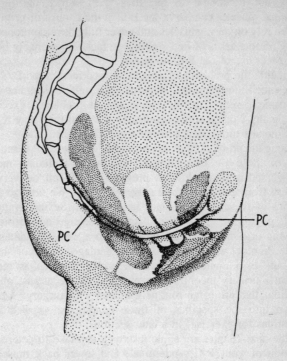

FIGURE 2   P-C Muscle

functions of the abdominal and the P-C muscles became, in a sense, reversed. This means that our P-C is now called upon to do a far harder job than it was originally 'designed' for, and thus it is crucial, especially for women, that this muscle be in topnotch condition.

Problems of a Weak P-C Muscle

Just as a muscle that is never exercised cannot be in good condition, the same is true of a muscle that is not used correctly. And the surprising fact is that a large percentage of women have never learned complete control of their P-C. This is so partly because the nerves that activate the P-C muscle do not fully develop until the second year of life (which is one reason a baby cannot be toilet trained any earlier—the muscles necessary for toilet training are

33

usually not functional in the first year). Since the thigh and abdominal muscles can assist the P-C in the control of urine, many children rely on these muscles and never fully develop proper use of the P-C. Some cases of bed-wetting, in fact, can probably be traced to incorrect use of the P-C muscle.

In adults, the problems of a weak or incorrectly used P-C muscle can be much more serious. But since this muscle does not show in any cosmetic sense, nor give evidence of problems, except indirectly, many women suffer needlessly when all they may require is what amounts to a reeducation of the P-C muscle.

Among the problems that can be caused by a weak P-C muscle are many of those we have already mentioned, including menstrual distress, bed-wetting, difficult pregnancy, difficult delivery, slow recovery from childbirth, and even infertility. We will go into the specifics of these problems in a later section. Sexual dysfunction, including painful intercourse, lack of feeling, and difficulty in achieving orgasm, can often be traced to a weak or damaged P-C muscle. In older women, a P-C that is damaged or out of shape can contribute to a number of medical problems, such as rectocele, cystocele, urinary incontinence, prolapse of the uterus, and other conditions that are often routinely treated with surgery. Again, we will go into the specifics of these conditions, as well as give suggestions for exercise, in a later section.

In the next chapter are some tests you can take to determine the condition of your P-C, abdominal, and lower back muscles. No matter what the results of the tests, remember that each of these muscles can be strengthened easily and quickly, and that the stronger they are, the better you'll feel and look.

4

Testing
Your Pelvic Power

Following are some simple tests you can take at home to determine how strong your pelvic muscles are. Remember when you take these tests that every woman is different: you may have relatively strong lower back muscles, for example, and a very weak P-C; or you might have a strong P-C but abdominal and back muscles that are out of shape. When you have taken the tests you will know which muscles you need to work on the most.

Whatever the results, bear in mind that the condition of any muscle can be readily improved with exercise; furthermore, even if your muscles are already in good shape, exercise will not only increase your strength but also improve your control of those muscles. As an already fit young tennis player said when she enrolled in one of Maria's classes, 'Sure, I'm in good shape. But I want to be the best I can possibly be.'

Pelvic Fitness Inventory

Before we go on to specific tests, here is a quick quiz you can take which will give you a rough idea of your own pelvic strength.

1. Lower Back and Abdomen

This could be called the Honesty Test. Put on a leotard or bathing suit (or nothing at all) and take a good look at yourself in a full-length mirror. Stand as you normally do, without 'sucking in your stomach' or making a conscious effort to stand up straight.

Observe yourself from the front and from the side, then ask yourself these questions:

Is your posture erect, or do you slump?
Does your stomach stick out?
Is there a marked curve in your lower back?
Do you often suffer from a nagging backache?

If the answer to any of these questions is yes, your pelvic muscles are not in as good condition as they might be.

2. P-C Muscle

Answer the following questions for a good idea of the present condition of your P-C muscle:

Do you sometimes have a problem with urine escaping when you exercise, laugh, or sneeze?
Do you ever have a feeling of 'slackness' in your vaginal area?
Do you ever experience pain or lack of feeling in sexual relations?
Has your partner ever mentioned that you feel 'loose' during sexual relations?

If the answer to any of these questions is yes, your P-C muscle almost certainly needs to be strengthened.

Pelvic Strength Tests

The following are more exact tests of minimal muscular fitness in each of the pelvic muscle groups:

1. Abdominal Muscles

POSITION: Lie on your back with your arms at your sides. Bend your knees and anchor your feet under a piece of heavy furniture (or ask someone to hold your feet down).
ACTION: With your hands behind your neck, slowly *roll* up off the floor until you are sitting up. If you can do this easily, your abdominal muscles are in at least adequate shape (without a doubt, however, exercise will make them stronger and firmer).

If you can't roll all the way up, don't despair. The abdominal muscles respond very quickly to exercise, and you will be amazed at the improvement you will see in just a few short weeks, including a flatter tummy, firmer midriff, and smaller, more supple waist.

2. Lower Back Muscles

You will need an assistant for this one.

POSITION: Lie on your stomach with your head resting on your hands, a folded towel under your waist.

ACTION: Ask your friend to hold down your upper back while you lift your legs (together and straight) up into the air and hold them for a count of ten. Don't worry about how high you lift your legs—the important thing is to hold the pose for ten seconds.

If you can pass this test, and most women can, your lower back muscles are in fairly good shape, but they too can be strengthened with exercise, resulting in improved posture and appearance.

Also, especially if this exercise was easy for you but the abdominal exercise wasn't—which is very common—your back muscles are too tight. Exercises for lower back flexibility will not only help streamline your figure but in conjunction with abdominal exercises will help bring your entire pelvic area into alignment, giving you better posture, more energy, and freedom from back-aches.

3. P-C Muscle

There are several tests you can take to determine the condition of your P-C muscle. The first should also be used as a periodic check on your progress as you do the exercises in our programme.

(1) P-C Control. When you are urinating, with your legs spread wide, try to stop the flow of urine completely. (*Don't* try this during your first urination of the morning, or if you have recently drunk a great deal of liquid.) If you can *completely* stop the flow several times, your P-C muscle is probably in very good shape. If you can't stop it completely even once, the muscle has poor tone and you should begin exercising it.

(2) P-C Strength. Sit or stand comfortably, your legs somewhat apart, and contract the P-C muscle. The way to do this is to imagine

that you are holding back the flow of urine or contracting your anal sphincter. Try *not* to contract your back, thigh, or stomach muscles while you do this. (If you have difficulty contracting your P-C muscle, see chapter 8 for more specific instructions.)

Now, contract the muscle as *strongly* as you can for a count of ten seconds. Use a stop watch or estimate by counting slowly: 'One thousand and one . . . one thousand and two . . .' etc. When you have reached ten, relax the muscle, then immediately contract it again as strongly as you can, holding the full contraction for another count of ten seconds. If you can do this ten times in a row without the force of the contractions diminishing, your P-C muscle is in very good shape (and will get even better if you exercise it!). The earlier in the series that the strength of the contractions diminishes, the weaker your P-C is.

(3) P-C Endurance. Sitting or standing comfortably with your legs somewhat apart, begin to contract your P-C muscle rhythmically, again as strongly as you can, relaxing as soon as the full force of a contraction is released, and immediately contracting again. The count goes like this: 'And *one* [contract] and [relax] *two* [contract],' etc.

If you can do fifty of these contractions without the full force of the contraction lessening, your P-C muscle is in good shape. If you can do 100, it's in excellent shape (and 100 is the aim). Remember that a *full* contraction is all that counts. As soon as you count and nothing happens, or the contraction is feeble, it's time to stop (but you will almost certainly do better next time).

If you can only do a few strong contractions, on the other hand, don't feel discouraged. The P-C responds very quickly to exercise. You will be surprised how many more full contractions you will be able to do in a few weeks.

In the next section of the book we will tell you everything you need to know to successfully follow the three Levels of our programme for pelvic health and fitness.

*Everything You Wanted to Know
about Exercise But Didn't Know
Whom to Ask*

The remaining chapters of this book show you how to achieve and
maintain pelvic fitness. Before we go on, however, we'd like first to
answer the question 'What *is* fitness?' so you'll know exactly what
you're doing and why it's guaranteed to work.

What is physical fitness?

There are *degrees* of fitness (probably stopping somewhere short
of 'total'), just as there are degrees of proficiency in sports. Each of
us is capable of achieving optimal fitness *for herself*, and what
constitutes optimal fitness for one woman may be very different from
the optimal fitness requirements of her sister. For example, if you
are a sixty-five-year-old woman who enjoys gardening and an
occasional outing to a nearby city, your needs will be very different
(and less) than those of a twenty-five-year-old Marine lieutenant.

In other words, the sixty-five-year-old woman will need to be fit
enough to enjoy good health and a reasonable level of energy, but
her life would not be made any more *effective* by the ability to, say,
run five miles in forty minutes. On the other hand, a fitness level that
allows running five miles without fatigue and provides a great deal of
physical strength might be crucial to the Marine. Obviously, the
women in our example would have to follow very different exercise
programmes to achieve their fitness goals.

What is the best way to achieve my fitness goals?

This depends on your goals. There are three different types of
fitness, which have different degrees of importance to overall body
health. They are aerobic, skeletal, and muscular. You must do

different types and amounts of exercise, depending on which sort of fitness you are trying to achieve.

What is aerobic fitness?

Aerobic fitness, also called cardiovascular fitness, refers to the strength and health of your heart and your circulatory system, although all parts of your body benefit from this sort of fitness. Aerobic exercises are any that raise the heart rate, cause sweating and vigorous breathing, and are done for a *sustained* period of time (twelve to twenty minutes, three to four times a week would be minimal). The most widely performed aerobic exercises are jogging, walking, swimming, and cycling. Jumping rope and aerobic dancing are suitable aerobic exercises, too.

Aerobic fitness is essential to your overall health, and we urge you to begin an aerobic programme if you are not now involved in one —perhaps with half an hour of walking a day. Because these exercises burn a significant number of calories, they are also the best kind for anyone who wants to lose weight. For more detailed information on beginning and maintaining an aerobic exercise programme, see the appendix.

What is skeletal fitness?

This type of fitness has to do with the health and flexibility of your joints. Flexibility can best be achieved by stretching exercises, such as yoga postures. Because they are not strenuous, flexibility exercises can be done every day.

While flexibility is desirable, especially to prevent stiffness with advancing age, these exercises do little to help you lose weight, and are usually performed as a supplement to other, more vigorous types of exercise.

What is muscular fitness?

This type of fitness refers to the strength and endurance of the muscles in your body. Weight training and calisthenic exercises promote this sort of fitness, and should be done three to five times a week.

While most exercises for muscular fitness will not lead directly to weight loss, they do lead to a slimmer appearance because while muscle tissue weighs *more* than fat tissue, it takes up *less* space. For example, saggy upper arms are usually the result of a combination of poorly conditioned muscles and too much fat. Exercises to improve

40

the strength of the muscles will help reduce the ratio of fat to muscle here, resulting in a slimmer, firmer appearance.

The programmes in this book are aimed at improving the fitness of the muscles in your pelvic area. Like any muscles in your body, including your heart, these can get out of shape; like all the other muscles, they can be rehabilitated with a regular programme of exercises.

Is muscle tone the same as strength?

Muscle tone refers to the state of your muscles when they are not working; a healthy muscle is always in a slight state of contraction and feels firm to the touch.

Muscular strength, on the other hand, is determined by the amount of work that muscle can do at one time. Lifting 100 pounds once shows strength. Endurance is indicated by the number of times or amount of time a muscle can perform work. If you could lift that same 100 pounds and hold it for fifteen minutes, or lift it several times in succession, this would be an indication of the endurance of your muscles used in the lifting.

How does exercise improve muscular fitness?

The only way a muscle can get stronger is by doing what it was designed to do: work. By the same token, muscles that do not work get out of condition. They become the opposite of toned; they become weak and flabby.

The most important thing to know is that, because it is their nature to work, *even weak and flabby muscles will become stronger when given the chance to perform work.* And the way to make them stronger is to give them more work to do than they are used to.

This can be done in two ways. First, you can get the muscles to move more weight than they are used to. Or you can work your muscles for a longer period of time than they are accustomed to working.

For example, suppose that you walk to work every morning carrying a briefcase that weighs ten pounds. This is the normal amount for you to carry, and your muscles are accustomed to carrying this much weight this particular distance. Now, if you want to improve your briefcase-carrying ability, you will have to ask your muscles to carry a little more weight than they are used to—but only a little. Too much might cause excessive fatigue, or injury, or actually be impossible for you.

41

Thus, in the briefcase example, you might add two pounds of books and begin carrying twelve pounds to work. *Or* you could carry the normal ten-pound load by a different, longer route. The point is that you get the muscles to do a little more work than they are used to —you give them an overload. The muscles in turn respond by growing stronger. Each time you add more overload they gain an increment of strength. Young mothers often notice this effect on their arms, which become gradually stronger as they carry a baby —who is slowly gaining weight.

Continuing to add to the weight or to increase the amount of time that your muscles work *are the only ways* to improve the condition of muscles. They are the reason any exercise programme, from weight training to running to the exercises in this book, works. A muscle must be challenged if it is to become stronger. It must be asked to do more than it is accustomed to, on a regular basis, and the extra load must be regularly increased.

What is maintenance?

When you have reached your fitness goal, and your muscles are at the desired level of strength, you can stop increasing the amount of work that you do. Instead, you continue to exercise, but at the goal, or maintenance, level. Maintaining muscular fitness is far easier than achieving it in the first place, and requires working out only two or three times a week.

What kinds of exercises will I be doing in the Pelvic Fitness Programme?

There are two types of exercise that challenge your muscles and cause them to grow stronger, and we will be using both of them in this programme. They are known technically as isotonic and isometric exercises. (There is a third type of exercise, which makes use of machines and is employed only in weight-training programmes.)

Isotonic exercises are any exercises in which you *move* your muscles, such as sit-ups or weight training. Isometric exercises are those in which you contract a muscle (squeeze it) but do not move it. The extra work your muscle does in an isometric exercise is provided by increasing the number of times you do the contraction or the amount of time that you hold each contraction. Clenching your fist is an example of an isometric exercise.

*

42

Keeping all this information in mind will help you stick with our exercise programme. This is especially true if you are starting out from very bad condition. The first time you do a given exercise you may feel hopeless, certain that you will never be able to reach your goals. Fortunately, your muscles will respond to the exercise no matter what your mind is thinking, and they will automatically adjust to the new challenge. In fact, although the results may not be immediately apparent, your muscles become a little bit stronger each time you exercise. Thus, if you conscientiously stick with the programme and do the exercises correctly and on a regular basis, you can't help but achieve the results you want, sooner or later (the more conscientious you are, the sooner).

Part Two

———

**Getting
Started**

6

Before You Begin

Starting an exercise programme, like beginning any worthwhile activity, requires some minimal preparation to ensure maximum success. Following are preliminary steps to take, including tips on how and where to exercise.

Get a Checkup

Before you begin our programme, you should have a medical checkup. While none of our exercises is particularly strenuous, strenuous is a relative term, and your doctor will best be able to advise you on your own capabilities. Furthermore, you should make sure that you don't have any underlying condition that would make exercise inadvisable for you at this time. Because this is a programme of *pelvic* exercises, we recommend that you get a thorough gynaecological exam before you start, and discuss your intentions with your doctor. If you wish, show her or him the exercises in this book. If your doctor feels that you should go easy on or even skip some of the exercises, by all means follow those instructions.

On the other hand, it is possible that your doctor may say that it's all right for you to exercise and yet discourage you from beginning the programme, perhaps pooh-poohing the possibility that you will get any results from it. If this is the case, and your doctor says that there is no *medical* reason not to exercise, feel free to go ahead. The fact is that a lot of doctors, while well aware that exercise can have dramatic results, have a feeling (based on experience) that many women do not have the willpower to perform exercises for a long enough period of time to get results.

'I always considered exercise a waste of time,' says a gynaecologist we know. 'But several of my recent patients have had good results in relieving their symptoms. I'd recommend it now if I felt the woman was motivated.'

Remember that only *you* can provide the motivation to stick with your exercises. When you return to your doctor for your next checkup in six months or a year, she or he will undoubtedly be pleased to see the progress you have made. In fact, your success may encourage your doctor, like the one quoted above, to recommend exercise to other patients who want to improve the condition of their bodies.

While we recommend a checkup for everyone, the more out of shape or the older you are, the more important it is. For example, if you have never got your shape back after bearing children, it is essential that the condition of your back and joints be checked out. If you have been sedentary for several years or are very overweight, any exercise programme will be more difficult and possibly more hazardous for you. Also, if you are now pregnant, pregnancy is not the time to *begin* a vigorous exercise programme of any sort. Many of the exercises in this book can be used to good effect by pregnant women, however, and there are special exercises for the pregnancy year later in the book.

Make a Schedule and Stick to It

The exercises in this programme (with the exception of some exercises which take only a few seconds each and should be performed daily), can be completed within five or at most ten minutes. For best results, the entire programme should be performed a *minimum* of four and preferably five times a week. You should not, however, exercise five days in a row. It is best to allow your body a little recovery time after two or three days of working out.

It's also important to exercise at around the same time each day, especially at the beginning. The time you choose depends on your own schedule and energy level. If you are a morning person who wakes smiling and ready for action, then you should exercise in the morning, even if it means getting up ten minutes early or giving up your second cup of coffee. If, on the other hand, you are the sort of person who can't even focus until you've been awake for an hour, schedule your workout for late afternoon or evening. If you can't always work out at the same time, it's all right to switch your workouts around *occasionally*, but for best results try to stick to your schedule as closely as possible.

This is important for at least two reasons. For one thing, if you know that you are always going to exercise at nine on Tuesday, Wednesday, and Thursday mornings, and consistently do so for several weeks, you will be less likely to find an excuse for skipping your routine 'just this one time.' The second reason is that your body itself becomes adapted to an exercise schedule, and begins to 'look forward to' the activity. By creating a routine for yourself, and following it from the beginning, you will quickly become familiar with the exercises and they will soon require less conscious effort on your part. Once you have been working out for a while and are used to the various exercises, you can be more flexible. Don't do this, however, until you are sure that the exercise has become a habit for you.

The importance of the 'habit' aspect of exercise is often overlooked. To see how it works, examine your own habit of brushing your teeth. Nobody was born regularly brushing her teeth—you simply do it without thinking. But when do you do it? Almost certainly at a particular time or times every day. After getting up and just before going to bed, for example. Or after every meal, if you are an especially conscientious brusher. Practically nobody, though, brushes her teeth sometimes in the morning after breakfast, on other days at two in the afternoon, and once in a while in the middle of the night.

No matter what your exercise schedule, *never* work out just after eating. If you've had a heavy meal, it's best to wait an hour or two; if you've had a lighter meal or snack, wait at least fifteen minutes. You should do this because when you exercise, the blood tends to concentrate in the muscles being exercised, and if there is food digesting in your stomach at the same time, that blood will be diverted. This can result in indigestion or even cramps, and is likely to make your exercises uncomfortable and less productive. Also, don't do all your exercises within an hour of bedtime, because the stimulation can keep you awake. (However, some women enjoy doing *relaxing* yoga postures before bed, as an aid in quickly falling asleep. There are several relaxation exercises in a later section.)

Find A Place

Some of the exercises in this programme can be done anywhere —in fact, no one else need know that you are doing them. Others require a flat space with plenty of room for you to lie down and move your body around.

If you have a full-length mirror in your house or apartment, try to arrange an exercise space in front of that. Not only is it easier to exercise correctly if you can see what you are doing, but as you begin to improve, your new, fitter body reflected in the mirror will provide extra motivation. If you tend to be very self-conscious about working out, and you don't want others to see you, a room with a lock on the door can be your own private gymnasium.

Wear Something Comfortable

The only consideration in deciding what to wear when exercising is comfort. And this means no tight, pulling clothes or belts. Leotards or bathing suits are ideal; shorts and a cotton T-shirt, especially if you tend to perspire heavily, make a good exercise outfit. Remember that you want something that will move with your body.

Be Prepared

Although no special equipment is required for the exercises in our programme, a tennis ball is optional for some of the more advanced exercises. When you get to that level of the programme, keep the tennis ball with your exercise clothes, or at least near where you work out so that you won't have to waste time hunting for it (and perhaps losing the impulse to work out).

Also, because some of the exercises will be performed lying on the floor (never on a bed—it's too soft to provide the support your body needs while working out), it is a good idea to buy or make an inexpensive exercise mat. Chain stores like Sears sell these for very little money, or you can make one easily by folding over a large towel or blanket, or simply using the pad from an outdoor chaise longue. A towel spread over a thick rug provides an ideal surface, but the bare floor will be uncomfortable for most women and downright painful for any woman who tends to be bony.

Warm Up

Although the exercises in this book are unlikely to cause any strain or injury, the chances are even further diminished if you warm up beforehand. Just as you would not expect your automobile to start right up on a cold morning without letting the engine get warm, so your muscles need a little preliminary activity to begin to work efficiently. In the next chapter are a series of very gentle stretching and movement exercises which should be done before you begin your pelvic exercises. The entire series takes only two to three minutes, and will leave your whole body feeling stretched, relaxed, and ready to go.

Choose Your Level

When we first began designing the Pelvic Fitness Programme, we realized that not all women would be starting from the same condition of fitness. Therefore, we have devised three separate levels of exercise for achieving pelvic fitness.

We created these programmes by thinking of three women we know, each at a very different fitness level and each with different needs.

The first woman we shall call Paulette. Paulette, in her mid-forties, has borne four children. Although she was active in her youth, she has not got any regular exercise in over twenty years. Paulette is troubled with backaches and the beginning of symptoms indicating poor pelvic fitness. She feels tired a great deal of the time and is increasingly distressed by flabby muscle tone and spreading hips and waist.

Because her youngest children are still at home, Paulette has limited time and resources. Furthermore, since she has not exercised in several years, she has doubts about her ability to stick with any but the most minimal exercise programme.

It is for Paulette and other women in poor condition, including those of middle age and older, that we have designed Level I of the Pelvic Fitness Programme. This Level is for anyone who is just beginning to exercise or is very overweight or in very poor condition. The exercises are sufficiently challenging to improve the

51

condition of the pelvic muscles, but not in any way exhausting or difficult. They are therefore ideal for any woman who wants tangible results with a minimum expenditure of time and energy.

Lucy, the second woman for whom we created a programme, is in her early twenties. Although she has not exercised since childhood, Lucy still retains the natural muscle tone and flexibility of youth. Lucy and her husband hope to have children in the next few years, and she therefore wants to build pelvic fitness. Because her job in the securities industry is demanding and time-consuming, however, Lucy has little time for exercise.

We have designed Level II for women like Lucy, who need to begin a quick and effective systematic exercise programme for the pelvic muscles, and who are starting from average physical condition. Not only will the exercises at this Level improve the strength of Lucy's pelvic muscles, they will also prepare her to go on to a more complete and strenuous exercise programme if and when she becomes ready.

Anita is a thirty-year-old athlete. She has always been active, playing tennis and golf since she was a child, and has always believed in the value of exercise. Two years ago she began running and now enters road races, some of them as long as ten miles. But Anita has noticed that she often has an aching back, and that as running strengthens the muscles of her legs she is becoming stiffer in the pelvic area. What Anita needs is a concentrated programme of exercises for the pelvic area that will not be time-consuming—she already devotes several hours a week to running—but will be challenging enough to enable her to improve the strength and endurance of her back and abdominal muscles, while also training the P-C muscle.

It is for Anita and others like her that we have designed Level III of the Pelvic Fitness Programme. Anita had been accustomed to performing as many as fifty sit-ups at one time; *she will be able to get similar results in much less time by following our shorter, more strenuous abdominal workout*. A bonus is that Anita's sex life will almost certainly improve as she learns super-control of the P-C and gains maximum flexibility of the entire pelvic area.

The three Levels of our Pelvic Fitness Programme are designed so that one of them will be ideal for you. If you want to begin to get into shape again, choose Level I, like Paulette. For the Lucys who are in adequate shape but want to improve general fitness, perhaps in preparation for pregnancy, Level II is right. And Level III provides advanced exercises for women who wish to progress beyond minimal pelvic fitness.

No matter what programme you choose, however, and no matter what your present level of fitness, you should master all of the basic exercises at Level I before moving on to a higher Level, because these exercises form the basis for some of the more advanced work.

Once you have chosen a Level, your goal will be to be able to perform all exercises on that Level at the maximum number of repetitions. And remember that there is nothing wrong with starting or remaining on an 'easy' Level. We all have different strengths and weaknesses, based on previous experience and heredity. You may find, for example, that you can easily do the Level II abdominal exercises at the highest number of repetitions, while the lower back exercises on that same Level give you trouble. If that is the case, simply perform the abdominal exercises at the *maximum* number of repetitions while you do fewer repetitions for your back—or even drop back to Level I exercises until your back has become stronger.

Likewise, it is not necessary for all women to progress to Level III. Some of the exercises at this level are very challenging, and may be too difficult for you, or you may not have the time or energy to devote to mastering them. But every woman will achieve much improved pelvic fitness by first mastering Level I and/or Level II and then continuing to perform our maintenance exercises.

Following some of the exercises for the abdomen and back are 'recovery' exercises. These exercises, which take only a few seconds, relieve any sense of strain or tension and help to maintain flexibility in the area being worked.

Remember that our *basic* exercises should take no more than five to ten minutes a day, including warm-ups. Some of the exercises must be performed more than once a day, *for only a few seconds each*. However, they are included in the total time. (At the beginning, while you are still learning the exercises, it may take you a little longer to do the whole routine.)

Some women will want to progress beyond minimal pelvic fitness. For this purpose there are special exercises presented in a later section for specific conditions, such as pregnancy, and for particular goals, such as improved sexual fitness. These exercises are to be performed *in addition to* the basic exercises. Obviously, this will increase your total exercise time, but in no case should it add more than a few minutes. In fact, once you have reached the maintenance programme, the total amount of time you will need to spend on pelvic fitness per week, even if you include several special exercises, will be twenty minutes or less!

On each Level, the exercises are presented in this order: abdomen, pelvic floor, back. Most of the pelvic floor exercises can be done anywhere and at any time, but it is important to follow exactly the order presented for the abdominal and back exercises, since they are designed to flow into one another and to exercise the muscles in the most efficient and comfortable way possible.

All exercises are given in the following format:

NAME OF EXERCISE

PURPOSE: The muscle or muscles being worked in the exercise.
POSITION: The *starting* position for the exercise.
ACTION: The movements that you will make (or the isometric contraction that you will hold). In some cases the action will be further broken down into numbered steps.
BREATHING: For some exercises, best results are obtained if you breathe in for one part of the movement and out for another. For other exercises, the instruction will say to 'breathe naturally.' The most important thing to note about breathing is that you should *never* hold your breath while performing exercises.
REPETITIONS/GOAL: This will tell you how many times to repeat the exercise. For example, "three times on the left side, repeat on the right.' For most, but not all, exercises there is an initial number of repetitions to perform when you are first beginning the exercises on that level, and a final number of repetitions that you will build to over a period of time. If you find any exercise too difficult at the suggested number of repetitions, don't worry about it. Do only as many as you can, and each time you exercise try to do one more. It is far better to do even one repetition of an exercise correctly and with control than to do twenty repetitions incorrectly.
TIPS: Reminders and suggestions to help you do an exercise properly or more easily. For example, in many exercises it is important (and sometimes difficult) to keep your shoulders relaxed; this reminder will be repeated in 'Tips.'

Progress Report

Following the exercises for each Level is a sample Progress Report, which summarizes the exercises required for that Level and includes a chart which you can copy to record the exercises you do each day.

7

Warming Up

Following are seven warm-up exercises, to be done before *all* the calisthenic-type exercises in Levels I, II, or III. Read through the instructions for all of these warm-ups before you begin. They should be done in exactly the order presented and should flow into one another as smoothly as possible. If you have a little trouble at first, don't worry about it. By your third or fourth exercise session, they will be familiar and easy.

Who Should Do Warm-ups: All women, whether on Level I, II, or III. These warm-ups can also be done at any time during the day when you are feeling stiff or sleepy, or have been sitting in one position for too long.

Tips for Warm-ups: When you are first learning these exercises, be careful not to overdo them, especially when bending or twisting movements of your trunk are required. Once you have learned the warm-ups, perform them as vigorously and rhythmically as possible without strain. The exercises will be easier and more enjoyable if you do them to music with a good strong beat.

1. STEPS

PURPOSE: To get your heart beating faster; to begin to loosen all parts of your body.
POSITION: Stand comfortably, arms at sides, your feet slightly apart and pointing ahead.
ACTION: Without going anywhere, walk in place, keeping your toes down and heels up, but not lifting your feet from the floor. This will look almost like a dance step, and should be performed rhythmically and vigorously.

BREATHING: Breathe naturally.
REPETITIONS: 40 times, alternating feet (20 steps on each foot). This will go very quickly.
   Go immediately to

FIGURE 3   Steps

2. SHRUGS

PURPOSE: To loosen your upper back and shoulders.
POSITION: Stand comfortably, arms at sides.
ACTION: Standing as relaxed as possible, make slow, exaggerated circles by shrugging your shoulders from the back to the front. Get as much movement as you can: when your shoulders rotate upward, try to lift them as high as your ears. After the forward shrugs, reverse direction and rotate your shoulders to the back.
BREATHING: Breathe naturally.
REPETITIONS: 4 circles to the front, 4 to the back. If your upper back feels very stiff, add another set of 4 and 4.

Go immediately to

FIGURE 4   Shrugs

3. CROSSES

PURPOSE: To improve circulation; to loosen entire upper body.
POSITION: Stand comfortably, arms straight up over your head.
ACTION: Keeping your arms straight and slightly behind your head, bring them toward each other and across, right wrist in front of the left wrist. Now move your arms outward and drop them freely to your sides. Immediately bring them back up in a wide circle and again across them (slightly behind your head), this time with the left

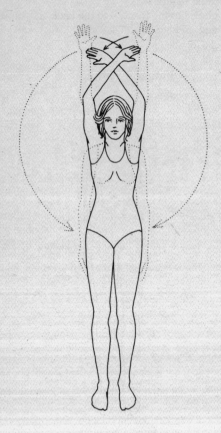

FIGURE 5   Crosses

60

wrist in front of the right. Repeat all motions, swinging your arms in vigorous, wide, rhythmic movements. It should look as if you are waving, trying to attract the attention of someone far away.

BREATHING: Breathe naturally.

REPETITIONS: 5 crosses with the right wrist in front, 5 with the left wrist in front, alternating.

  Go immediately to

4. PULLS

PURPOSE: To improve circulation, to loosen legs and hips.

POSITION: Stand comfortably, arms relaxed.

ACTION: Keeping your back straight, shift your weight to your left leg and raise your right knee toward your chest, pulling it as high as possible with your hands. (Don't worry if you can't lift it very high at first.) Hold for two counts ('one [pull] . . . two [hold] . . .

FIGURE 6   Pulls

61

three [hold] . . .'), then lower it. Shift your weight to your right
foot and repeat with your left knee.
BREATHING: Breathe naturally.
REPETITIONS: 4 times with each leg, alternating.
   Go immediately to

5. BENDS

PURPOSE: To improve circulation; to stretch side trunk muscles.
POSITION: Stand comfortably, arms at your sides, fingertips lightly
brushing the sides of your thighs.
ACTION: Without twisting your trunk, bend directly to the right side
as far as you can *comfortably*. Let your fingertips slide down your
right thigh as you do so. Immediately return to upright position and

FIGURE 7   Bends

repeat. This will look like a gentle bouncing movement. Repeat, this time to the left side.

BREATHING: Breathe naturally.

REPETITIONS: 8 times to each side, alternating. If you still feel stiff, repeat with 4 times to each side; then 2 to each side.

TIP: *Don't* overdo the side bending, especially at first. Bend only as far as you can without strain.

Go immediately to

6. KICKS

PURPOSE: To improve circulation and increase hip flexibility.

POSITION: Stand comfortably, arms at your sides.

ACTION: Point your right foot out to the side and slide the toe along

FIGURE 8   Kicks

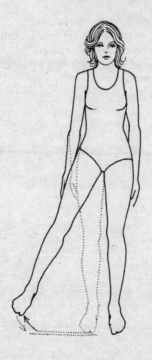

63

the floor and then up six to eight inches into the air. Return to start and continue, kicking rhythmically. Repeat with left leg.

BREATHING: Breathe naturally.

REPETITIONS: 5 to each side.

Go immediately to

7. TWISTS

PURPOSE: To loosen the front, back, and sides of your trunk.

POSITION: Stand comfortably, arms outstretched at shoulder height to the front. Imagine that you are holding a broom stick in your hands.

ACTION: Keeping arms outstretched and a couple of inches apart, twist your entire trunk to the right, your arms moving with it (the right arm will be stretched to the right side, the left arm crossed to the right over your trunk). Swing back to centre and then to the left. Repeat rhythmically.

BREATHING: Breathe naturally.

REPETITIONS: 5 times to each side, alternating.

TIPS: Do not perform this exercise too vigorously, but rather gently, feeling the stretch in your trunk as you move.

When you have completed these warm-ups, it is time to begin the exercises on Level I, II, or III.

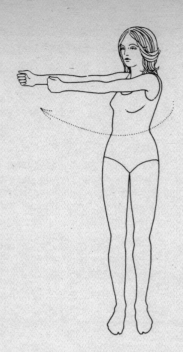

FIGURE 9   Twists

SUMMARY OF WARM-UPS

WARM-UP	REPETITIONS
1. Steps	40, alternating feet
2. Shrugs	4 front, 4 back
3. Crosses	5 each side, alternating
4. Pulls	4 each leg, alternating
5. Bends	8 to each side, alternating
6. Kicks	5 to each side
7. Twists	5 each side, alternating

Level I Exercises

When you have mastered Level I:
• you will be able to isolate (contract separately) the lower, middle, and upper abdominal muscles
• your abdominal muscles will be tighter and stronger, and your abdomen will begin to appear flatter and firmer
• you will be able voluntarily to contract your P-C muscle, resulting in better urinary control and more feeling during sexual relations
• your entire pelvic area will be more flexible, resulting in better posture and more comfort when standing and sitting
• you will be able to contract your buttock muscles separately, and your derriere will begin to tighten

This chapter contains the exercises for the first stage of the Pelvic Fitness Programme. All of these exercises are very safe and will be easy for most women. However, since some of them make use of isometric contractions (see chapter 4), they will require a little practice.

No matter what your current level of fitness, it is important to master all the exercises in Level I. The amount of time this takes will vary depending on your current level of conditioning and your experience with exercises. For some women, Level I will be mastered in just a day or two; for others it may take weeks or even months. It doesn't matter how long it takes; the important thing is to continue to do the exercises on a regular basis. As long as you do that, you will definitely see dramatic improvement, regardless of your present level of fitness.

Who Should Do Level I Exercises: Everyone participating in this programme, even women currently in good physical condition.

How long to Remain on Level I: This will vary, depending on your present condition. When you have mastered the maximum number of repetitions for each of the exercises and when you feel confident about your ability to perform the isometric contractions as pre-scribed, move on to Level II, performing those exercises at the lowest number of suggested repetitions. If this proves very difficult, return to Level I until you are stronger.

Abdomen

1. STOMACH PULL

PURPOSE: To strengthen and isolate the lower, middle, and upper parts of your abdominal muscles.
POSITION: This exercise can be done sitting, standing, or lying on your back. It does not need to be performed in the same position each time you do it, but can simply be done whenever you think of it.
ACTION: (1) Place your fingertips lightly on your pubic bone (the hard bone located near the top of your pubic hair). Now contract your lower abdominal muscles (or at least try to). If you cannot isolate this part of the abdomen, 'pull in your stomach' as strongly as you can until you feel some movement in the lower abdomen where your fingertips are touching. Hold the contraction as strongly as possible for a slow count of four, then
   (2) *Without releasing the contraction,* place your fingertips on the navel area and contract the central part of your abdominal muscles (this should be easier). Contract as strongly as possible for a slow count of four, then
   (3) *Without releasing the previous contractions*, place your fingertips on your abdomen directly under your rib cage, and contract the upper muscles as strongly as you can. Keep your shoulders relaxed while you lift *in* and *up*. Imagine that you are trying to press your midriff against your spine. Hold as strongly as possible for a slow count of four, then

68

(4) Relax your muscles from top to bottom, slowly, but without counting. As you do so, try to let the muscles go with control rather than just letting them 'hang out.'

BREATHING: Breathe naturally.

REPETITIONS: Do the entire series of contractions 5 times each time you do it, as often during the day as you remember to. Do it at least 3 times a day.

TIPS: This exercise may seem difficult at first because you are not used to isolating the different parts of your abdominal muscles. In fact, you may be totally unable to contract these muscles separately. Just continue to practice, *imagining* that you are isolating the muscles. With a few days' practice it will become easier, and you should begin to see results in terms of strength and tone, and eventually you will gain control over the muscles. Remember to do this exercise not only when you are performing the rest of the exercises in the Level I group but also at other times throughout the day. See chapter 12 for tips on exercising at other times.

Isometric exercises work better if they are performed with *full intensity* several times a day. When you contract any muscle, even if you can barely feel the contraction, try to hold it 100 per cent. Although you will be doing this several times a day, remember that each performance, no matter how intense, takes only a few seconds.

Finally, use of your fingertips in this exercise is important for two reasons. The first, obviously, is to allow you to feel when the muscle is contracting, and thus give you a greater awareness of the muscle movements. Second, use of your fingertips aids in concentration and, quite apart from the help it gives you in feeling the contractions, should allow you to focus your attention better on the muscles you want to move. If you think of your fingertips as a 'concentration point,' the exercise is easier to perform.

2. LITTLE ARCH

PURPOSE: To strengthen all abdominal muscles and improve flexibility of the pelvic area.

POSITION: Lie on your back, arms at your sides, both knees bent, chin pressed down toward your chest. The most important thing about this position is that your entire back, from head to buttocks, should be firmly supported by the floor. Make sure that the back of the head, the back of the neck, the upper and lower back all touch the floor. It may be necessary to bend your knees at a sharper

69

FIGURE 10   Little Arch

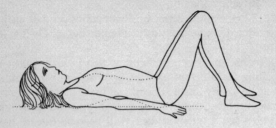

angle and consciously push your pelvis downward in order for your lower back to touch the floor.

ACTION: Maintaining the position outlined above, inhale and arch your back *slightly* as you do. Immediately exhale and push your spine down against the floor. Hold this position for a slow count of 6 while you exhale, forcing your lower back and buttocks against the floor and contracting your stomach muscles as strongly as you can.

REPETITIONS/GOAL: 4 times at first. Adding 1 repetition at a time, work up to 8.

BREATHING: Breathe in when you arch up, exhale as you press your lower back against the floor. Continue to push your back against the floor until you have exhaled completely; try to make this exhalation last for 6 counts.

TIPS: Your back is only slightly arched in the first part of this exercise, and the contraction into the floor should be rather strong. Remind yourself to keep your shoulders relaxed as you do this exercise.

3. HEEL PUSH

PURPOSE: To strengthen the entire abdominal area, with particular emphasis on the upper abdomen.

POSITION: Lie on your back, arms at your sides, your legs straight.

ACTION: Slowly bend your right leg, keeping the heel in contact with the floor and sliding it toward your buttocks. At the same time lift the upper part of your torso and try to touch your right knee with your left hand. If you cannot reach the knee, don't worry about it; just raise as high as you can (just lifting your head off the floor works the

70

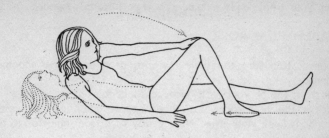

FIGURE 11   Heel Push

upper abdominals). When you have touched your knee, slowly return to starting position. Repeat on the opposite side.

BREATHING: Exhale when you raise your body, inhale while you lower it.

REPETITIONS/GOAL: Start with 2 on each side, alternating; work up to 4.

TIPS: It is not necessary to bring your heel more than part way toward your buttocks. When performing this exercise try to keep the movements slow and controlled—never strain. You will notice a slight improvement each time you do this exercise.

4. ARMS OVER

PURPOSE: To stretch the lower back and strengthen the lower abdomen.

POSITION: Lie on your back, your knees slightly bent, your arms outstretched on the floor behind your head.

ACTION: Inhale. As you exhale, raise your right arm and left leg toward the ceiling. Keep your head on the floor and your knees slightly bent. Now try to touch your left leg with your right hand. You can touch it anywhere from knee to toe—the important thing is to lift the leg as high as possible. Inhale as you return to starting position. Repeat with the opposite arm and leg.

After completing one lift with each leg, push the small of your back into the floor and stretch your whole body before repeating.

BREATHING: Exhale up, inhale down.

REPETITIONS/GOAL: Start with 4 on each side, alternating; work up to 8 per side.

TIPS: If you feel a sense of strain in your back, flex your knees more. Keep your whole body relaxed as you perform this exercise.

5. ABDOMINAL ROCK

PURPOSE: Recovery; to relieve any sense of strain in your abdomen or back.
POSITION: Lie on your back, arms and legs relaxed.
ACTION: Pull both knees close to your chest, cradling them against your body with your arms. Now gently rock from one side to the other.
BREATHING: Breathe naturally.
REPETITION: 4 'rocks' to each side, or more if needed for relaxation.

NOTE: If you found all of these abdominal exercises easy, you may go on to Level II abdominal exercises. If the isometric contractions in Exercise 1, the Stomach Pull, were new to you or more difficult than the strength exercises, continue to do the Stomach Pull until it is easy for you to isolate and contract the three parts of your abdominal muscles.

Pelvic Floor

The exercises that follow *are the basic exercises for the pelvic floor*, and should be mastered before you move to the more difficult ones. These exercises may seem strange to you if you have never done them before, but they can be mastered by any woman and will become natural and almost automatic after a while.

All pelvic floor exercises are based on the 'Kegel contractions,'

FIGURE 12   Abdominal Rock

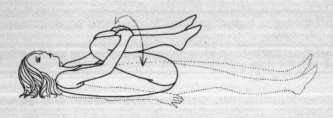

which were developed by the late gynaecologist Arnold Kegel in the 1950s for use by his patients with different degrees of relaxation (weakness) of the P-C muscle. The test in chapter 2 to rate the condition of your P-C muscle made use of these contractions. If you had any difficulty with that test, or did not try it, here is the best way to become familiar with Kegel contractions.

First, imagine that you are trying to hold back the flow of urine. Squeeze as tightly as you can. The muscle you move in that squeeze is the P-C muscle. With practise, you will be able to distinguish various parts of the muscle and to add greatly to the force of each contraction.

If you have difficulty squeezing by imagining that you are holding back the flow of urine, it may help to practise the P-C contraction while you are urinating: try to stop the flow several times during urination (but not during your first urination in the morning). If you don't succeed in stopping the flow but only slow it somewhat, that is fine. The most important thing in this stage of the programme is to become aware of your P-C and how it feels when you are contracting it. You may notice that your abdominal and/or thigh muscles contract at the same time. Again, don't worry about this. The ultimate goal is to gain control of the P-C without the aid of other muscles, and just becoming aware of the muscle itself is an important first step.

Although P-C contractions can be performed in any position, you may find it easier at first if you perform them while you are lying down, with your legs spread lightly apart. When you are certain that you can voluntarily contract the P-C muscle, begin to perform the exercises as outlined.

Some women, no matter what the condition of the rest of their bodies, have a P-C muscle that is naturally very strong and in good tone. If you are lucky enough to have such a P-C muscle, you can still benefit from the exercises in this programme, increasing both your strength and control.

1. FAST CONTRACTIONS

PURPOSE: To gain control and improve the strength of the P-C muscle.
POSITION: This exercise can be done sitting, standing, or lying down (see above). It need not be performed in the same position each time, but can simply be done whenever you think of it.

ACTION: Forcefully contract your P-C muscle, slowly release it, then contract strongly again. Do this as quickly as you can, to a count: '*One* [squeeze] and [relax] *two* [squeeze] and . . .' In the beginning, your count may be quite slow, but you will quickly pick up speed as you gain more experience with the exercise and improve the strength of your P-C.

BREATHING: Breathe naturally. Do not hold your breath, and do not worry about coordinating your breathing with the contractions. (Though you may, if that is easier for you.)

REPETITIONS/GOAL: Do 20 contractions each time you do this exercise. Do these as many times during the day as you remember to. A minimum would be 5 times a day, but even more would be better. Your progress will be fastest if you do a minimum of 200 contractions during the day (this would be 10 times total).

TIPS: Remember that you want to contract as strongly as possible each time, and that when you release the muscle you want to relax it as fully as possible. Your first efforts may seem feeble to you because you may have lost much of the tone of the muscle. If that is the case, just continue, contracting as forcefully as you can. If you are conscientious and do this many times during the day you will see (feel) definite improvement within a short time (six weeks at most).

The best time to do your first Kegel contractions of the day is first thing in the morning, just after you wake up, while you are still relaxed. To make sure you remember to do this, tell yourself over and over just before you go to sleep that this is the first thing you will do when you wake up. You might also tape a note near your bed where you will see it when you open your eyes. After a while, doing the contractions when you wake up will become automatic.

2. P-C HOLD

PURPOSE: To increase strength and control of the P-C muscle.

POSITION: Standing, sitting, or lying down. See Exercise 1.

ACTION: Slowly contract the P-C muscle until you are squeezing it as forcefully as you can, then hold the contraction for a slow count of 10. Just as slowly, relax the muscle.

BREATHING: Breathe naturally. Do not hold your breath.

REPETITIONS: 10 times (this makes a total of 100 counts). If you find that you are unable to maintain a strong contraction for more than a few counts, then just do as many full contractions as you can (even if it's only 2 or 3) and try to add another every day or so.

Tips: When doing slow contractions, it is easy to let the abdominal muscles 'assist' your P-C. To find out if you are doing this, place your fingertips on the lower part of your abdomen while you contract your P-C and note if there is a tightening. If so, spread your legs a little and try to work the P-C without help (but don't worry if you can't do this at first).

3. PELVIC FLEX

PURPOSE: This exercise will increase the flexibility of the entire pelvic area. Once you have mastered it, other contractions will be added to the basic movement.

POSITION: Kneel on the floor, your buttocks on your heels, your toes straight and your hands on top of your knees. Round your back and drop your head, relaxing your neck and allowing your chin to fall close to the chest.

ACTION: There are two parts to do simultaneously. Practice them separately.

(1) Inhale fully, then exhale, at the same time pulling your entire stomach in and upward. Imagine that the pull of the muscles starts at your inner thighs, and you are lifting everything you can move between the knees and rib cage.

(2) At the same time you contract your stomach muscles, tilt your pelvis toward the back. This involves 'tucking' your buttocks muscles downward. To do it correctly, you might imagine that the 'bowl' of your pelvis is filled with water, and you want to spill a little of that water behind you. Another way to imagine this movement is to pretend you are inspecting a seam in your leotard or

FIGURE 13   Pelvic Flex

75

pantyhose at the inner thigh near the groin: lift your pubic area while forcing your buttocks down into your heels. If you are doing this movement correctly, you may feel a pulling along the tops of your thighs.

To combine steps (1) and (2): inhale, then exhale, pulling your stomach in and upward and tilting your pelvis to the back. Hold this position for a count of 5, then slowly return to starting position.

BREATHING: Exhale on contracting, inhale while relaxing.

REPETITIONS/GOAL: Begin with 4 contractions; work up to 8 by adding 1 every few days or every week.

TIPS: Keep your shoulders relaxed throughout this exercise. You may feel some discomfort in kneeling on your feet. This discomfort should vanish with a few attempts but if it doesn't, you may do this exercise standing, as follows:

ALTERNATE POSITION: Stand, your feet 1 or 2 inches more than shoulder width apart, your knees slightly bent, your hands resting on the tops of your thighs. Your back should be rounded, your neck relaxed, and your head dropped forward.

ACTION: Perform the two parts of the exercise as in the kneeling position.

Lower Back

1. BUTTOCKS SQUEEZE

PURPOSE: This exercise will help strengthen your entire lower back area and improve your control over the individual muscles.

POSITION: Lie on your stomach, your legs together, your head resting comfortably on your hands.

ACTION: This is another isometric exercise. Squeeze your buttocks together, as forcefully as you can, then relax the contraction. Immediately squeeze again. Do this rhythmically, to a count of: '*One* [squeeze] and [relax] *two* [squeeze] and . . .'

BREATHING: Breathe naturally; don't hold your breath.

REPETITIONS/GOAL: Start with 30, or as many as you can do *fully* contracting the muscles. Work up to 50 rhythmic, full contractions (50 sounds like a lot, but this goes very quickly).

TIPS: This is a very safe and effective exercise for the lower back. You will see the best results if you really concentrate on each squeeze, putting '100 per cent' into it.

FIGURE 14   Knee Pull

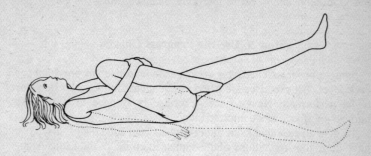

2. KNEE PULL

PURPOSE: This exercise will build some strength in the lower back, but its primary purpose is to increase flexibility in this area where many women are very tight.

POSITION: Lie on your back, legs outstretched, arms at your sides.

ACTION: Slowly bend your right knee, bringing it toward your chest. As soon as you can reach it, clasp your hands around it and 'hug' the knee to your chest. Relax and return to starting position, then repeat with the left leg.

BREATHING: Exhale as you bring the leg up, inhale as you lower it.

REPETITIONS/GOAL: Begin with 4 pulls each side, alternating; adding 1 per week, work up to 8 per side.

3. CAT BACK

PURPOSE: Recovery; to ease any sense of strain in your lower back.

POSITION: Get down on the floor on your hands and knees, your arms and legs no wider apart than your shoulders.

ACTION: (1) Inhale, and at the same time lift your head high and look upward while dropping your spine toward the floor (as if you were a 'swaybacked' horse). Hold for 3 counts, then (2) Exhale, and exactly reverse the above position: lower your head, arch your back, contract your stomach muscles, as if you were trying to push your stomach against your spine. Hold for 6 counts, then repeat (1) and (2).

REPETITIONS: Perform the Cat Back 3 times.

TIPS: After you feel confident with the basic movement, you may add a contraction of the P-C muscle and of the buttocks to part (2) for further benefits to the entire pelvic area. Do this exercise gently and gradually, and never to the point of discomfort.

How to Use the Progress Charts

Sample progress charts for you to copy and use are provided for each level. All exercises are listed on the charts in the order they are to be performed. Next to each exercise is a space to record the number of times you completed it.

To give an example from the Progress Chart for Level I: after you have done four repetitions of Abdomen Exercise 2, the Little Arch, simply write '4' in the space *next to* the Little Arch and *below* Day 1, Week 1. For the exercises that must be performed several times a day, simply place a small dot or *x* in the space each time you perform the exercise.

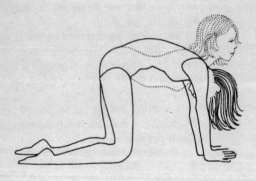

FIGURE 15   Cat Back

SUMMARY OF EXERCISES

Level I

ABDOMEN	BEGINNING REPETITIONS	GOAL
1. Stomach Pull	5, 3 times a day	same
2. Little Arch	4	8
3. Heel Push	2 each side, alternating	4
4. Arms Over	4 each side, alternating	8
5. Abdominal Rock	4 each side	same

PELVIC FLOOR		
1. Fast Contractions	20, 5 times a day	20, 10 times a day
2. P-C Hold	10	same
3. Pelvic Flex	4 each side	8

LOWER BACK		
1. Buttocks Squeeze	30	50
2. Knee Pull	4 each side, alternating	8
3. Cat Back	3	same

PROGRESS CHART LEVEL I

Exercise		Start/ Goal	WEEK 1					WEEK 2					WEEK 3					WEEK 4				
			Day 1	Day 2	Day 3	Day 4	Day 5	Day 1	Day 2	Day 3	Day 4	Day 5	Day 1	Day 2	Day 3	Day 4	Day 5	Day 1	Day 2	Day 3	Day 4	Day 5
ABDOMEN																						
1. Stomach Pull	Isomet.	5, 3× Day																				
2. Little Arch		4/8																				
3. Heel Push		2/4 ea. side																				
4. Arms Over		4/8 ea. side																				
5. Abdominal Rock		4 ea. side																				
PELVIC FLOOR																						
1. Fast Contractions		20 × 5 20 × 10																				
2. P-C Hold	Isomet.	10																				
3. Pelvic Flex		4/8																				
LOWER BACK																						
1. Buttocks Squeeze	Isomet.	30/50																				
2. Knee Pull		4/8 ea. side																				
3. Cat Back		3																				

80

9

Level II Exercises

When you have mastered Level II:
• your side abdominal muscles will be suppler and firmer, resulting in a better-toned waist and midriff
• your entire abdominal area will be much stronger, firmer, and flatter
• you will be able to isolate (contract separately) the lower, middle, and upper parts of your P-C muscle
• your increased P-C control will further improve urinary control and sexual functioning
• the insides and outsides of your thighs will be stronger and firmer
• you will have increased control and firmness of your buttocks muscles as well as improved strength and flexibility in your lower back

The following exercises build on and are more challenging than the exercises on Level I. If you have not yet mastered the Level I exercises for the pelvic floor, do so before starting the pelvic floor exercises in this chapter.

Who Should Do Level II Exercises: Anyone who has mastered the exercises on Level I; that is, who can perform the maximum number of repetitions for each category of exercise without difficulty or sense of strain. For many women, particularly those who have always worked out regularly, this may take only a day or two. For others, particularly those who are overweight or very out of shape, it may take as long as six weeks or more.

Who Should Not Do Level II Exercises: Anyone who has not mastered the exercises on Level I; anyone who is very obese or very out of shape; anyone who continues to have a great deal of difficulty with the Level I exercises; anyone who is now pregnant and has not been working out previously.

How Long to Remain on Level II: This will vary, depending on your present condition. For most women, it will take about six weeks to master the exercises on this Level. When you can easily do the maximum number of repetitions for each of the exercises, you may either move on to Level III, performing the new exercises at the lowest number of suggested repetitions, or you may move into the Level II Maintenance Programme. The Maintenance Programme, which is described in chapter 11, consists of three exercises, to be performed three times a week (except for the pelvic floor exercise, which must be performed every day). Continuing to perform these maintenance exercises indefinitely will assure you a good continuing level of pelvic fitness.

Remember to do your warm-ups before exercising!

Abdomen

1. KNEE ROLL

PURPOSE: To strengthen your abdominal muscles, with special attention to the oblique (side, or waist) muscles.
POSITION: Lie on your back, arms outstretched at shoulder level, palms turned down to the floor.
ACTION: Bend your legs and bring both knees as close to your chest as you can. *Keeping your arms and shoulders on the floor*, roll your knees to the right side as far as you can (you may or may not be able to touch the floor). Return the knees to centre, then roll them to the left.
BREATHING: Breathe naturally, in time with your action.
REPETITIONS/GOAL: Start with 4 rolls to each side, alternating; work up to 8 each.

FIGURE 16   Knee Roll

RECOVERY: Finish by bringing both your knees to your chest and hugging them there with your arms. Briefly bring your head up to touch the knees, then relax and stretch your entire body out along the floor, reaching for the wall behind you.

TIPS: When performing the rolls, keep your knees as close to your chest as possible. Don't worry if you can't touch the floor with your knees at first; this will come with practice. Keep your shoulders on the floor throughout the 'roll' part of the exercise.

2. ROLL-DOWN

PURPOSE: This exercise is good for the entire abdominal area, and prepares you to do more strenuous sit-ups.

POSITION: Sit on the floor with your knees bent in front of you, your feet close together. Your hands are behind your head, your chin on your chest.

ACTION: (1) Slowly, deliberately, roll down to the floor, trying to feel your spine unwind, vertebra by vertebra. The lower part of your back touches the floor first, then the middle, the upper, and last of all your head. When you finish, you are lying on your back with your legs still bent.

(2) To return to starting position, straighten and spread your legs, then slide to sitting position with your hands pushing against the

floor to help you. Bend your knees in front of you for another roll-down.

BREATHING: Exhale while you roll down, inhale, exhale back up.

REPETITIONS/GOAL: Start out doing 4 roll-downs; add 1 every few days or week till you have built to 8.

TIPS: This exercise is very safe, even for women with back problems. If you have no back problems and find the exercise easy, you can add to the difficulty (and increase your abdominal strength) by substituting the following for step (2) above:

(2) Roll-up: This is a bent-legged sit-up, done in a manner just opposite that of the roll-down. Instead of spreading your legs when you return to starting position, keep your legs bent, cross your hands across your chest, and slowly, vertebra by vertebra, roll up off the floor until you have reached starting position. Hold a moment, then do another roll-down.

BREATHING: Exhale while you roll up, inhale, then exhale down.

REPETITIONS: Start with as many as you can do slowly and with control. When you have built to 8 roll-ups and roll-downs, it is time to move on to more challenging abdominal exercises, either on Level III or the Maintenance Programme.

FIGURE 17   Roll Down

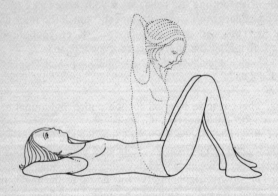

3. SIDE SIT-UP

PURPOSE: To further strengthen your side abdominal muscles, with special attention to the upper abdominals.

POSITION: Lie on your back, legs spread as far apart as possible, your right arm to the side of your body and your left arm crossed over your body, the left hand grasping top of the right wrist.

ACTION: Keeping your legs and your hands on the floor, raise your torso slightly and twist it toward the right. Sliding your hands along the floor, try to touch your right foot with your hands (it doesn't matter if you can't quite reach it). You will come nearly to sitting position but not quite. Uncurl, returning to starting position. Repeat, twisting toward the left.

BREATHING: Exhale when you curl up, inhale when returning to starting position.

REPETITIONS/GOAL: Start with 4 on each side, alternating; add 1 more every week until you build to 8.

TIPS: It is important to do this on a smooth surface, such as a wooden floor; otherwise your body will not move smoothly as you 'follow' your hands with your torso toward your foot. Remember to keep your legs on the floor at all times and to keep your right hand (with left resting on it) on the floor and fairly close to your body.

Curl toward your foot only as far as you can reach comfortably; you will improve with practice.

FIGURE 18   Side Situp

4. PELVIC SLANT

PURPOSE: Relaxation and recovery.
POSITION: Lie on your back, your legs bent with knees together, your hands at your sides, palms down.
ACTION: Inhale, and at the same time lift your derriere in the air as high as it will go until your back is straight, slanting down toward your head. Your head and shoulders remain on the floor. Hold for a slow count of 6, then return to start.
BREATHING: Breathe naturally; don't hold your breath.
REPETITIONS: Do this twice.
TIPS: If you still feel discomfort or strain in the lower back, follow this with 1 or 2 repetitions of the Abdominal Rock (Abdominal Exercise 5, Level I).

Pelvic Floor

1. FAST CONTRACTIONS (See Pelvic Floor Exercise 1, Level I)

PURPOSE: To increase control and strength of pelvic floor.
POSITION AND ACTION: This exercise is the same as the Fast Contractions (Pelvic Floor Exercise 1) on Level I. At Level II your aim is to increase the speed with which you rhythmically contract and release your P-C muscle, and also to increase the force of each contraction.
REPETITIONS: Begin with 30 repetitions, noticeably faster and more intense than those you were doing on Level I; work up to 40, at least 5 times a day.

FIGURE 19   Pelvic Slant

2. P-C ISOLATION

PURPOSE: The purpose of this exercise is to begin to learn control over all parts of the P-C muscle. This will almost certainly seem difficult (but not strenuous) at first, but it will become easier as you continue to practise it.

Before you begin, it will help to visualize the vaginal canal, which is not a hollow tube. It is, rather, more like an oblong balloon with no air in it; the sides touch each other as the sides of a collapsed balloon touch. To perform the exercise, imagine that you are trying to close a long seam. First, button the bottom part (sphincter), then gradually pull the open zipper higher, closing each part of the 'seam' in order. The more you concentrate and try to visualize, the better you will be able to feel the separate areas.

POSITION: Any comfortable position, with legs slightly apart.

ACTION: This exercise consists of contracting the pelvic floor for a total of 8 slow counts. It should be done in stages, as follows

(1) Concentrate on the vaginal sphincter, the outermost part of the P-C, which is the easiest part to visualize and control. Contract the sphincter for 2 counts. Hold the contraction, then

(2) Contract the lower part of the vaginal canal for 2 counts. Continue holding the two previous contractions, then

(3) Concentrate on the middle part of the vaginal canal, and squeeze it together for 2 counts. Hold the three previous contractions and

(4) Concentrate on the topmost part of the vaginal canal and contract it for 2 counts.

(5) Slowly release all contractions in order, from the top to bottom, but without counting.

BREATHING: Breathe naturally; don't hold your breath.

REPETITIONS/GOAL: Begin with 2 complete sets of contractions 3 times a day; adding 1 complete set every few days, work up to 5 complete sets of contractions 3 (or more) times a day.

TIPS: Isolating the parts of the P-C may seem impossible at first, but it will become much easier as you gain familiarity with and control over your P-C muscle. You will master the exercise sooner if you use your imagination as an aid: re-read the description of the vagina and really try to visualize what you are attempting to do, even if you can't *feel* any difference in the location of the contraction.

3. BALL PULL

PURPOSE: To increase control of all the pelvic muscles together; to improve the strength and tone of the inner thighs.

POSITION: Sit on the floor with your knees bent in front of you. Place a tennis ball (or other soft ball, or even a rolled pair of very bulky socks) between your knees and squeeze hard enough to hold it there. Place your hands on top of your knees, then lean back, extending your arms fully. This will look something like a jackknife position. If you find that you are unable to maintain your balance in this position, it's all right to drop your hands to the floor and support your weight on your hands. The exercise will not work on your stomach muscles as vigorously as in the first position, but you will obtain all the other benefits.

ACTION: (1) Round your back, dropping your chin toward your chest, and squeeze the ball between your knees. At the same time, try to bring your inner thighs as close together as possible. When you are squeezing as forcefully as you can with knees and inner thighs,

(2) Contract your P-C muscle. Without releasing the previous contractions,

(3) Contract your abdomen in three stages: first the bottom part,

FIGURE 20　　Ball Bounce

88

then the centre, then the top. Hold all contractions together for a count of 8, then slowly release in reverse order.

REPETITIONS/GOAL: Start with 1 complete set of contractions; add 1 a week, building to 3.

TIPS: Make sure your shoulders are relaxed throughout this exercise.

Imagination will also help. Try to imagine, as you add contractions, that you are trying to draw the ball from between your knees, down your thighs, and up your abdominal area to just under your rib cage. With each contraction, the ball will go higher and higher in your imagination. When you finally release, imagine that the ball is travelling slowly back down, by the same route, bringing with it relaxation to your stomach, P-C, inner thighs, and knee area.

Lower Back

1. BUTTOCKS SQUEEZE WITH BALL

PURPOSE: To strengthen and isolate the muscles of your lower back, with special attention to the buttocks. This exercise also works your P-C muscle and helps firm the outer and inner thighs.

POSITION: Lie on your back, your legs straight, your hands at your sides. Place a tennis ball (or rolled pair of thick socks) between your knees.

ACTION: (1) Squeeze the right buttock as strongly as you can, holding the contraction for a slow count of 5. Relax slowly, then contract the left buttock, again holding for a slow count of 5. Continue to alternate, squeezing left, right, etc., 10 times each side.

(2) With the tennis ball still between your knees, contract both buttocks strongly with a snapping motion and force your lower back against the floor. Hold a brief moment, relax, then snap again.

BREATHING: Breathe naturally; don't hold your breath.

REPETITIONS/GOALS: Part (1) 10 times each side, alternating. Part (2) 8 times; add 1 every few days until you reach 16.

TIPS: Holding the ball between your knees increases the force of the contractions, and also works the outer thighs and has some effect on the pelvic floor. However, the alternating buttocks squeeze can be done in any position without the ball and is an excellent toning exercise for the derriere; performing it frequently whenever you think about it will increase the firmness and improve the shape of your backside.

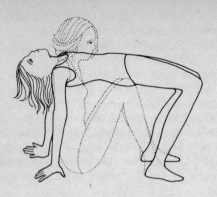

FIGURE 21 Hip Bounce

2. HIP BOUNCE

PURPOSE: To promote flexibility in the lower back and help firm the abdomen. Bonus: this exercise helps strengthen and firm the upper arms.

POSITION: Sit on the floor with your knees bent and together, the lower part of your legs slightly apart (there should be 4 to 5 inches between your feet). Your hands are on the floor beside you, in line with your shoulders, your fingers pointing away from you to the back.

ACTION: Drop your head back and lift your buttocks as high as you can until your trunk is in a straight line. All your weight is now

FIGURE 22 Knee Stretch

90

supported on your hands and feet. Lower your trunk, then repeat.
BREATHING: Exhale as you raise your trunk, inhale as you lower it.
REPETITIONS/GOAL: Start with 4 bounces; add 1 a week until you work up to 8.

3. KNEE STRETCH

PURPOSE: Recovery; to stretch out the lower back.
POSITION: Sit on the floor, your knees bent in front of you and a few inches apart.
ACTION: Put your palms together, then stretch them forward between your knees, reaching as far forward as you can without discomfort (this may be quite far if you are naturally flexible, or barely past your knees if you are somewhat stiffer). Return to starting position and repeat.
BREATHING: Exhale as you stretch forward, inhale as you return to start. Do not hold your breath.
REPETITIONS: Do 8 stretches, then rest with your back rounded and your head on your knees.

4. ALTERNATE LEG LIFT

PURPOSE: To strengthen the entire lower back area.
POSITION: Lie on your stomach, hands under your head, your face comfortably to one side.
ACTION: (1) Without arching your back, lift your right leg straight up, then lower it and lift your leg. Continue to alternate until you have lifted each leg 4 times.
   (2) Repeat, but when you reach the highest position with your right leg, hold it for a count of 8. Lower, then repeat with the left leg.
BREATHING: Breathe naturally.
RECOVERY: Roll back on your knees, your buttocks resting on your heels, your arms stretched forward on the floor and your head close to or on the floor. Hold until all sense of strain is gone.
REPETITIONS/GOALS: Part (1) begin with 4 lifts on each side, alternating; work up to 8 per side. Part (2) begin with 4 on each side, alternating; work up to 8 on each side.
TIPS: When you lift either leg, make sure that your pubic bone remains in contact with the floor. It is not necessary to lift your leg very high for either position; far more important is to lift it even a

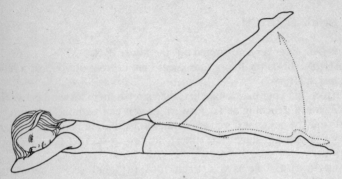

FIGURE 23   Alternate Leg Lifts

few inches from the floor and keep your back straight. If you feel any sense of strain in your lower back as you perform this exercise, check to make sure that your back is not arching.

5. LEG PULL

PURPOSE: To strengthen the lower back, stretch the front of the thighs, and help ensure proper pelvic alignment.

POSITION: Lie on your stomach, your legs straight, your arms comfortably at your sides, your head raised slightly.

ACTION: Bend your right leg. At the same time slightly lift your trunk and reach for the right foot with both hands. If you can reach your foot (or any part of the leg), grasp it and pull it upward as high as you can, then hold for 6 counts. Let the foot go, and repeat with the opposite leg.

BREATHING: Breathe naturally.

REPETITIONS/GOAL: 2 pulls with each leg, alternating; add 1 per week to each side until you can do 4 each.

TIPS: If you can't reach your foot or even the leg, just keep trying; if you still can't reach it after you have performed this several times, ask for assistance. If you feel a sense of strain in your lower back when you have finished this exercise, follow it with the recovery position used for Exercise 4, the Alternate Leg Lift.

SUMMARY OF EXERCISES

Level II

ABDOMEN	BEGINNING REPETITIONS	GOAL
1. Knee Roll	4 each side, alternating	8
2. Roll-down	4	8
3. Side Sit-up	4 each side, alternating	8
4. Pelvic Slant	2	same
PELVIC FLOOR		
1. Fast Contractions	30, 5 times a day	40, 5 times a day
2. P-C Isolation	2, 3 times a day	5, 3 times a day
3. Ball Pull	1	3
LOWER BACK		
1. Buttocks Squeeze with Ball	(1) 10 each side, alternating	same
	(2) 8	16
2. Hip Bounce	4	8
3. Knee Stretch	8	same
4. Alternate Leg Lift	(1) 4 each side, alternating	8 each side
	(2) 4 each side, alternating	8 each side
5. Leg Pull	2 each side, alternating	4 each side

PROGRESS CHART LEVEL II

		Start/Goal	WEEK 1					WEEK 2					WEEK 3					WEEK 4				
Exercise			Day 1	Day 2	Day 3	Day 4	Day 5	Day 1	Day 2	Day 3	Day 4	Day 5	Day 1	Day 2	Day 3	Day 4	Day 5	Day 1	Day 2	Day 3	Day 4	Day 5
ABDOMEN																						
1. Knee Roll		4/8 ea. side																				
2. Roll-Down		4/8																				
3. Side Sit-Up		4/8 ea. side																				
4. Pelvic Slant		2																				
PELVIC FLOOR																						
1. Fast Contractions		30/40 5 × Day																				
2. P-C Isolation	Isomet.	2/5 3 × Day																				
3. Ball Pull		1/3																				
LOWER BACK																						
1. Buttocks Squeeze ~ Ball	Isomet.	(1) 10 ea. side (2) 8/16																				
2. Hip Bounce		4/8																				
3. Knee Stretch		8																				
4. Alternate Leg Lift		4/8 ea. side																				
5. Leg Pull		2/4 ea. side																				

10

Level III Exercises

When you have mastered Level III:
• your entire abdominal area, including midriff, waist, and lower abdomen, will be strong and firm
• you will have good control over all pelvic muscles, working separately and together
• your P-C will be strong and supple, giving you increased control and feeling during sexual relations
• your entire pelvic area will be flexible and toned, resulting in better posture and a slimmer appearance
• your inner and outer thigh muscles will be stronger and firmer, and the backs of your legs and lower back will be more flexible

The following exercises are much more challenging than the exercises on Level II. If you have not yet mastered all the Level II exercises, do so before starting the exercises in this chapter.

Because Level III is an advanced programme, not all women will want or need to move on to it. In general, this is a programme for highly motivated women who are in good health and who have no underlying back condition or other problems that would make it difficult to stick to a strenuous programme. For many women, the Level II programme followed by Level II Maintenance will provide a good degree of continuing fitness for all the muscles of the pelvic area.

Who Should Do Level III Exercises: Anyone who fits the description above and who has mastered the exercises on Level II; that is, anyone who can perform the maximum number of repetitions for each category of exercise without difficulty or sense of strain.

Who Should Not Do Level III Exercises: Anyone who has not mastered the exercises on Level II; anyone who is obese or out of shape; anyone who continues to have a great deal of difficulty with the Level II exercises; anyone who is now pregnant and has not been working out previously.

How Long to Remain on Level III: You should continue to do these exercises on a regular basis (four or five times a week) until you can perform all of them at the maximum number of repetitions with no difficulty and no sense of strain. For most women proceeding to this Level, this will take three to eight weeks. When you have mastered the exercises in this programme, you may proceed to the Level III Maintenance Programme, which is described in the next chapter.

Because the exercises are so much more strenuous than those on Level II, we recommend that you rest for thirty seconds between sets of exercises, especially when you are just beginning this Level or any time you feel a strain. This is particularly important for the abdominal exercises. Instead of or in addition to the pause between sets, you can relieve any sense of strain by briefly performing the abdominal recovery exercise, the Pelvic Slant (Abdominal Exercise 4, Level II).

Note: If you have a great deal of difficulty performing the exercises in Level III, spend more time on Level II before returning to this Level.

Remember to warm up before working out each time you exercise.

Abdomen

1. ABDOMINAL BOUNCE

PURPOSE: To strengthen the upper part of your abdomen.

POSITION: Sit on the floor with both knees bent in front of you. Place your hands on your upper thighs so that the fingertips just touch but do not overlap the knees.

ACTION: (1) Keeping your back straight, lean back slightly, allowing your hands to slide back about 2 inches. You should now be sitting with your trunk at about a 45-degree angle with your thighs.

(2) Keeping your back straight, move your trunk forward a few inches until your fingertips are once again just even with the tops of your knees. Immediately repeat both movements, bouncing rhythmically.

REPETITIONS/GOAL: Start with 8 bounces; add 2 bounces every other day until you work up to 30.

BREATHING: Breathe naturally; don't hold your breath.

FIGURE 24   Abdominal Bounce

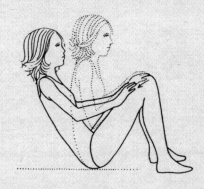

97

TIPS: Keep your shoulders relaxed throughout and be sure not to let your fingertips go over the tops of your knees during part (2) of this exercise. If you are doing it correctly, you will feel a pulling in your upper abdomen. If the exercise seems easy, move your feet closer to your knees for a greater challenge.

RECOVERY: Pull your chest close to your knees, briefly arch your back and drop your head back, then immediately round your back and rest your head on your knees for a few seconds until any sense of strain is gone.

2. V-SIT

PURPOSE: To strengthen all parts of your abdomen, with special attention to the lower abdominal muscles; it also helps strengthen your thigh muscles.

POSITION: Lie on your back with your hands lightly resting on your thighs, your legs together.

ACTION: Slowly and with control raise your trunk, sliding your hands along your thighs and up your legs, reaching toward your ankles. *At the same time* raise your legs. Stop when your torso and legs are at the same height, each at about a 45-degree angle with the floor. Slowly return to resting position.

BREATHING: Exhale as you lift your torso and legs, inhale as you lower them.

REPETITIONS/GOALS: Start with 4; add 1 every few days until you can do 8.

FIGURE 25   V-Sit

TIPS: This is a rather strenuous exercise; if you have great difficulty doing it you may substitute the Roll-up from Level II (Abdominal Exercise 2), building the number gradually to as many as 30.

3. SIDE SIT-UP

PURPOSE: To strengthen your oblique (side) abdominal muscles.
POSITION: Lie on your back, your legs spread apart, your knees bent. Your right arm should be resting on the floor a few inches from your body and to the side; your left arm is crossed over your body, your left hand grasping your right wrist.
ACTION: The action of this exercise is very similar to that of the Side Sit-up on Level II (Abdominal Exercise 3). Slowly curl your trunk up on the right side, at the same time sliding your hands along the floor close to the body and reaching for your right foot. You may not be able to reach the foot at first; simply curl up as far as you can. Slowly return to starting position and repeat on the left side.
BREATHING: Exhale as you curl up, inhale as you return to start.
REPETITIONS/GOAL: Begin with 4 sit-ups on each side, alternating; add 1 per side every week or two until you have worked up to 8 on each side.
TIPS: Keep your hands close to your body as you twist up. Your trunk should not be raised very far above the floor.

FIGURE 26   Side Situps

99

4. BODY RAISE

PURPOSE: To strengthen all of the abdominal muscles.

POSITION: Sit on the floor with your legs straight and together, your hands folded behind your head.

ACTION: Pull your stomach muscles in, drop your chin to your chest, and *slowly* lean back to the floor. *At the same time* lift your legs off the floor. When your eyes and your feet are at the same level, hold for a slow count of 5, then return to starting position.

BREATHING: Exhale as you drop your body and lift your legs; at all other times breathe naturally. Do not hold your breath at any time.

REPETITIONS/GOAL: Do this exercise 1 time at first; add 1 repetition every week or two until you can do 4 with complete control.

TIPS: This is the most difficult of the abdominal exercises and may be a strain at first. If you find it too difficult, spend more time on the Roll-ups (Abdominal Exercise 2, Level II) until your abdominal muscles are stronger. To make the exercise even more challenging (and therefore more beneficial), you can perform it with your arms straight out overhead.

This exercise should always be followed by

RECOVERY: (1) Lie on your back, pulling your knees close to your chest, and hug your legs to your body. Lift your head off the floor and rock from side to side several times, then rock backward and forward. (If you have a very bony spine and rocking forward and backward is painful, you may omit this step.)

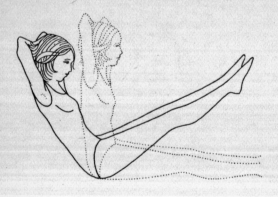

FIGURE 27   Body Raises

(2) Finish by sitting up in tailor position (with your legs crossed in front of you). Clasp your hands behind your back, then raise your arms behind you, at the same time dropping your head back and leaning your trunk backward. Immediately drop your hands and bring them to the front while you curl your back forward and drop your head to the floor. Rest in this position with your hands in front of your head, until all sense of strain is gone.

Pelvic Floor

1. FAST CONTRACTIONS

PURPOSE: To further increase strength and control of pelvic floor.
POSITION AND ACTION: This exercise is the same as the Fast Contractions on Levels I and II. The goal is to increase the speed with which you rhythmically contract and release your P-C muscle, as well as to increase the force of each contraction.
REPETITIONS: Begin with 40 repetitions, noticeably faster and more intense than those you were doing on the Level I programme. Work up to 60 fast contractions, 5 times a day.

2. P-C ISOLATION

PURPOSE: The purpose of this exercise is to increase your control and awareness of all parts of the P-C muscle. As you continue to practice, you will achieve better muscle tone and blood circulation throughout the entire pelvic region, as well as increased sensitivity in the nerve endings in this area.
POSITION AND ACTION: This exercise is the same as the P-C Isolation on Level II (Pelvic Floor Exercise 2), except that you should increase the holding of each contraction by 1 count. In other words, since you are holding 4 separate contractions, the total count will be 12: hold the sphincter contraction 3 counts; the lower part of the vagina 3 counts; the middle part 3 counts, and the upper part 3 counts.
REPETITIONS/GOAL: Begin with 4 complete repetitions 3 times a day; increase to 8, at least 3 times a day and whenever you think about it.

3. PELVIC TILT

PURPOSE: To improve tone and flexibility of the entire pelvic area; to strengthen the thighs.

POSITION: Kneel on the floor, sitting back on your heels with the tops of your feet pressed against the floor, your back straight, your arms slightly bent.

ACTION: Place a tennis ball between your knees. Take a breath, then exhale, at the same time lifting your hips off the knees, tilting the pelvis (as if you were trying to spill water behind you from the lip of the 'bowl' of your pelvis), rounding your back and thrusting your arms forward with your chin down toward your chest.

Practice this movement several times until you have mastered it. It will look and feel like a vigorous thrusting forward of your entire pelvic area. When you feel you have control of the basic movement, add a vigorous contraction of the pelvic floor at the moment that you thrust forward and hold the contraction along with the forward thrust for a slow count of 8.

BREATHING: Breathe naturally; do not hold your breath.

REPETITIONS/GOAL: Begin with 4 and add 1 a week until you have built up to 8.

TIPS: While performing this exercise, concentrate on achieving free movement of the pelvis, which is very rigid in most women. Use of the ball is not necessary, but increases the force of the

FIGURE 28   Pelvic Tilt

contractions. During all parts of the exercise, keep your upper body, particularly your shoulders, relaxed.

If you find bearing the weight of your body on the tops of your feet too painful, you can perform this exercise standing, very much as in the alternate position for the Pelvic Flex, (Pelvic Floor Exercise 3, Level I).

Lower Back

1. FORWARD BEND

PURPOSE: To promote flexibility in your lower back and in the backs of your thighs.
POSITION: Sit on the floor with both legs straight out in front of you and together.
ACTION: (1) Inhale and lift both arms toward the ceiling, stretching your palms upward. Hold the stretch a moment. Your head should be

FIGURE 29   Forward Bend

between your arms and you should feel a pulling from your neck to your lower back.

(2) Exhale, slowly bending forward *from the base of the spine*, keeping your back straight. That is, don't round the upper part of your back, but continue the stretch you started in the first part. Stretch in this position as far as you can (and it may not be very far at all), then

(3) Drop your arms to the floor, relax your upper body, and continue to bend forward (at this point you will be rounding your upper back). Bend forward as far as you can, ideally until your head touches your knees.

Hold the furthermost position without strain for a count of 6, then return to starting position.

BREATHING: Inhale on (1), then exhale until you have reached the limits of the initial stretch. Breathe naturally as you continue to bend forward and rest. Don't hold your breath.

REPETITION/GOAL: Begin with 1; add 1 a week until you are doing 3.

TIPS: This is adapted from a yoga position. If you have ever done yoga, you know that the goal is to stretch only as far as you can with comfort. You should never force a stretch, and in this sort of exercise you should not bounce. If you practice regularly, each time you exercise you will be able to bend a little further forward.

If you are experiencing marked discomfort, or you do not seem to be able to increase the degree of your forward bend, return to the Knee Stretch, (Lower Back Exercise 3, Level II) until your back is more flexible. If, on the other hand, this position is easy for you, you can increase the degree of the stretch by attempting to rest your chin on your knee and holding longer.

2. ADVANCED LEG PULL

PURPOSE: To strengthen the lower and upper back; to stretch the thigh and chest muscles.

POSITION: Lie on your stomach with your arms stretched out in front of you, your legs straight.

ACTION: (1) Bend your right leg, reaching for your foot with your left hand.

(2) Inhale, and as you do, lift both your head and right arm as high as you can, while at the same time pulling your right knee off the floor with your left hand. Raise your torso as you do so, if it is easier. Lift the leg as high as you can. Hold the extreme position for a count of 6, then return to start. Repeat on the other side.

BREATHING: Breathe naturally; don't hold your breath.

REPETITIONS/GOAL: Begin with 2 lifts on each side, alternating; add 1 on each side every other week until you reach 4 per side.

RECOVERY: Roll your body back until your torso is resting on your thighs, your knees bent, your hips over your heels. Stretch your arms forward with your head close to the floor and relax until there is no sense of strain.

FIGURE 30   Advanced Leg Pull

3. BACK CURVE

PURPOSE: To strengthen your upper and lower back.

NOTE: This exercise is extremely strenuous—don't even try it until you can easily perform the maximum number of repititions for all Level II lower back exercises. If you have a back problem, don't do this exercise at all, but substitute the Alternate Leg Lift, (Lower Back Exercise 4, Level II).

POSITION: Lie on your stomach, your hands at your sides, your legs a few inches apart.

ACTION: Slowly, with control, lift your head, arms, and legs off the floor. Your hands are stretched backward, as if reaching toward the backs of your knees. Lift your trunk and legs as high as you can *without strain*. Hold for a count of 5, relax, and return to resting position.

BREATHING: Breathe naturally; don't hold your breath.

REPETITIONS/GOAL: Begin with 1; add 1 every two weeks until you can perform 3.

TIPS: Because this exercise is so strenuous, recovery is especially important. After performing the Back Curve, *always* go immediately to the following exercise.

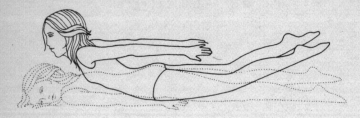

FIGURE 31   Back Curve

4. BACK SLANT

PURPOSE: Recovery. This position is also good for stimulating blood flow throughout the pelvic area, and is often effective in providing relief from menstrual cramps.

POSITION: Kneel on your hands and knees on the floor, as if for the Cat Back (Lower Back Exercise 3, Level I).

ACTION: Bending your elbows, place your forearms on the floor in front of you, at right angles to your body, your fingertips overlapping one another. Slant your back downward, resting your head on the floor in front of your arms. Try to get your chest to the floor, but keep your derriere high. Hold this position until all sense of discomfort or strain has vanished.

BREATHING: Breathe naturally.

REPETITIONS/GOAL: 1 time, following the Back Curve or whenever you need relief from discomfort in the lower back.

FIGURE 32   Back Slant

107

SUMMARY OF EXERCISES

Level III

ABDOMEN	BEGINNING REPETITIONS	GOAL
1. Abdominal Bounce	8	30
2. V-sit	4	8
3. Side Sit-up	4 each side, alternating	8 each side
4. Body Raise	1	4

PELVIC FLOOR		
1. Fast Contractions	40, 5 times a day	60, 5 times a day
2. P-C Isolation	4, 3 times a day	8, 3 times a day
3. Pelvic Tilt	4	8

LOWER BACK		
1. Forward Bend	1	3
2. Advanced Leg Pull	2 each side, alternating	4 each side
3. Back Curve	1	3
4. Back Slant	1	same

PROGRESS CHART LEVEL III

Exercise		Start/ Goal	WEEK 1					WEEK 2					WEEK 3					WEEK 4				
			Day 1	Day 2	Day 3	Day 4	Day 5	Day 1	Day 2	Day 3	Day 4	Day 5	Day 1	Day 2	Day 3	Day 4	Day 5	Day 1	Day 2	Day 3	Day 4	Day 5
ABDOMEN																						
1. Abdominal Bounce		8/30																				
2. V-Sit		4/8																				
3. Side Sit-Up		4/8 ea. side																				
4. Body Raise		1/4																				
PELVIC FLOOR																						
1. Fast Contractions		40/60 5 × Day																				
2. P-C Isolation	Isomet.	4/8 3 × Day																				
3. Pelvic Tilt		4/8																				
LOWER BACK																						
1. Forward Bend		1/3																				
2. Advanced Leg Pull		2/4 ea. side																				
3. Back Curve		1/3																				
4. Back Slant		1																				

109

Why Maintaining Pelvic Fitness Is Really Easy

'The exercises were hard the first few months,' says Nona, who has taken exercise classes with Maria for two years. 'I kept wondering if it was worth so much work. But then I found out how easy it is to *stay* in shape. I wouldn't stop now for anything.'

Nona has discovered a secret about exercise that for some reason is seldom mentioned in fitness books and classes: once muscular fitness is achieved, maintaining it takes relatively little time and effort. Weight lifters, for example, once they have attained their goals, need work out as infrequently as once every week to ten days —although to achieve that strength in the first place they must lift weights several times a week. (This principle does not, by the way, apply to aerobic exercises, which you must perform at least three times a week in order to maintain the benefits.)

Furthermore, another fact that is not generally known is that once you have worked up to a good level of muscular fitness, if for any reason you have to stop working out for a while—through illness, say, or a long vacation—you won't have to start at the beginning again. In fact, you maintain up to 70 per cent of the strength you have achieved for as long as a year. Of course you wouldn't start again at the same level at which you left off—this could lead to fatigue and even injury—but neither do you have to return to square one.

What we mean to tell you here is that once you have got this far, most of the battle is over. While you may continue to perform the exercises you have mastered at Level II or Level III, most women will probably prefer to switch to the Maintenance programme, in which it is necessary to work out only three times a week; furthermore, each workout consists of only three exercises, which will take you less than five minutes a day—or a total of fifteen minutes a week!

Of course we are not recommending that you confine your physical activity to fifteen minutes a week. Rather, now that you have proved to yourself that you are capable of greatly increasing your own pelvic fitness, it is our hope that you will be ready to engage in other exercises to improve the fitness of your entire body. (Most important, as we have pointed out elsewhere, is aerobic fitness.) This is a perfect opportunity to use your extra time and energy for a class in yoga or martial arts, or to take up or return to a sport. If you prefer to continue home exercises, add another routine —perhaps weight training or calisthenics—to your pelvic workout. Remember that the most important thing is to continue to let your body do what it most needs: be active.

Maintenance Programmes

The Levels of our programme for pelvic fitness are designed in a series of progressions, with the expectation that most women will master the most advanced number of repetitions for each exercise on each Level, and then begin the exercises on the next Level. However, we realize that not all women will be sufficiently motivated to move from Level I to Level II, and we therefore include here a minimal maintenance programme for Level I.

You may stay at this Maintenance Level indefinitely; however, you may also, at any time that you want to increase your pelvic fitness, decide to move on to Level II. Before you do so, make certain that you can easily perform the maximum number of repetitions for each exercise on Level I.

Level I Maintenance Programme

The Level I Maintenance Programme consists essentially of continuing to do the entire Level I programme, but decreasing the number of times the programme is performed to 3 a week (except for the isometric Stomach Pull, Abdominal Exercise 1, and the Slow Contractions, Pelvic Floor Exercise 1, which you should continue to perform daily).

Do not decrease the number of times you work out until you have mastered the maximum number of repetitions for each exercise.

112

Warm-ups:

Perform all warm-ups before exercising *every time* you work out (except for isometric workouts).

ABDOMEN	REPETITIONS	FREQUENCY
1. Stomach Pull	5	at least once a day
2. Little Arch	4	3 times a week
3. Heel Push	4 each side, alternating	3 times a week
4. Arms Over	4 each side, alternating	3 times a week
5. Abdominal Rock	4	3 times a week

PELVIC FLOOR		
1. Slow Contractions	10	once a day

Once you have mastered the P-C Hold and Fast Contractions, you can best maintain your strength by performing 10 *maximum* contractions and holding them for 6 full seconds. The best time to do this is first thing in the morning, before you get up.

2. Pelvic Flex	8	3 times a week

LOWER BACK		
1. Buttocks Squeeze	50	3 times a week
2. Knee Pull	8 each side, alternating	3 times a week
3. Cat Back	3	3 times a week

Level II Maintenance Programme

Level II, being a more advanced programme, has a far more challenging maintenance programme than Level I. Any woman who feels she doesn't have the time or energy to engage in a more strenuous programme will find that Level II Maintenance provides a good level of continuing pelvic fitness. Moreover, these exercises make an excellent supplement to any aerobics programme, particularly jogging or walking.

You may elect to continue on Level II Maintenance indefinitely; if at any time you choose to begin the Level III programme, return to the Level II basic programme for at least one week, making sure that you can comfortably perform all of the exercises at the maximum number of repetitions.

This maintenance programme, and that for Level III, should be performed 3 times a week, except for the pelvic floor exercises, which should be done every day. Furthermore, there will be a periodic testing every six weeks. Since you may eventually become bored with the exercises, we have suggested alternate exercises that you may occasionally substitute for the abdominal and lower back exercises.

Warm-ups:

Perform all warm-ups before exercising *every time* you work out (except for isometric workouts).

Abdomen

Roll-up. If you have been performing the Roll-down (Abdominal Exercise 2) only for the abdomen, now is the time to begin practising the Roll-up, which is a form of bent-legged sit-up, and is given as an alternate for step (2) of the Roll-down.

It is extremely important to perform this exercise exactly as it is described in chapter 9; traditional straight-legged sit-ups not only can strain your back, they may also be ineffective, since they do not 'isolate' the stomach muscles sufficiently.

How to go to maintenance: Reduce your performance of all exercises to 3 times a week, but when you get to Abdominal Exercise 2, the Roll-down, focus your attention on the Roll-up rather than returning to sitting with your legs spread. Your goal is to build to 15 of these sit-ups combined with a controlled Roll-down 3 times a week. If you have been doing the sit-ups all along, you can now do 8; add 2 a week until you can do 15. At this point you can discontinue the other abdominal exercises except for periodic testing, which will be explained below.

Pelvic Floor

The maintenance exercise for the pelvic floor is the same as for Level I: 10 maximum contractions, held for 6 seconds each, every day.

114

Lower Back

The maintenance exercise for the lower back is identical with Level II Lower Back Exercise 4, the Alternate Leg Lift. To go to maintenance, continue with all back exercises 3 times a week, and add 2 leg lifts per side every week until you are able to do 15 on each side, alternating; this is the maintenance level. Remember to follow this exercise with a recovery pose, such as the Cat Back (Lower Back Exercise 3, Level I).

Periodic Testing

It is obvious that the amount of exercise you will be performing on the maintenance programme is a good deal less than the exercise you did on the basic programme; as we mentioned before, it is much easier to maintain strength than it is to build it. But it is also obvious that not as many muscles are involved in the maintenance programme; for example, the Bent-legged Sit-up works the side abdominal muscles less directly than the Side Sit-up.

For this reason, the maintenance programme includes periodic testing, which consists simply of setting aside a longer-than-usual exercise period one day every six weeks, in which you will attempt to do each of the exercises in Level II at the maximum number of repetitions. If you find any of the exercises difficult to do correctly at the suggested number of repetitions, return to the full Level II programme (but only three times a week) until you have regained your former level of strength and flexibility.

Summary of Level II Maintenance Programme

	REPETITIONS	FREQUENCY
Warm-ups	All exercises as given in chapter 7	3 times a week
ABDOMEN		
Roll-up and Roll-down	15	3 times a week
PELVIC FLOOR		
Slow Contractions	10	once a day
LOWER BACK		
Alternate Leg Lift	15 each side, alternating	3 times a week
Cat Back	3	3 times a week

MAINTENANCE RECORD LEVEL II

Exercise		Reps.	WEEK 1			WEEK 2			WEEK 3			WEEK 4			WEEK 5			WEEK 6		
			Day 1	Day 2	Day 3	Day 1	Day 2	Day 3	Day 1	Day 2	Day 3	Day 1	Day 2	Day 3	Day 1	Day 2	Day 3	Day 1	Day 2	Day 3
Roll-Up/Roll-Down		15																		
P-C Slow Contractions		10 daily																		
Alternate Leg Lift		15 ea. side																		
Cat Back		3																		

* Once every six weeks, test your pelvic fitness by performing all exercises in Level II at the maximum number of repetitions.

116

A sample chart is provided on page 116 for you to keep track of maintenance; it is very important to record each workout, since you will be doing so few of them and you won't want to skip any.

Level II Maintenance: Alternate Exercises

From time to time you may wish to substitute alternate exercises for the abdominal and lower back exercises; not only will this keep you from getting stale, it will also help to exercise different muscles in different ways. Feel free to substitute the following exercises either occasionally, or for a week or two at a time.

Abdomen

Alternate 1. Side Sit-up (Abdominal Exercise 3, Level II).
REPETITIONS/GOAL: Begin with 8 on each side, alternating; add 2 on each side every week until you can do 15 per side.

Alternate 2. Chair Sit-up. This variant of the bent-legged sit-up is more challenging for many women.
PURPOSE: To maintain strength of the abdominal muscles.
POSITION: Lie on your back with your knees bent and your lower legs resting on the seat of a chair. If possible, hook your feet under the back of the chair. A folding bridge chair is ideal for this exercise, but you can use any chair (or stool) of approximately the same height (the higher the chair seat from the floor, the more difficult this exercise is). Your lower back should be *flat* against the floor (if necessary, check with a finger), your arms should be folded across your chest, and your chin should be tucked into your chest.
ACTION: Slowly curl up off the floor until you are nearly sitting; then slowly uncurl, as in the Roll-down, trying to feel your back unwind vertebra by vertebra.
BREATHING: Exhale as you curl up, inhale, then exhale down.
REPETITIONS/GOAL: Begin with as many as you can do, which will probably be somewhat fewer than your maximum repetitions of the Roll-up; add 1 Chair Sit-up a week until you can do 15, 3 times a week.
TIPS: This exercise is most effective if you perform it slowly and with control—don't 'jerk' up, and take care that your body does not twist to the side as you come up.

117

Lower Back

Alternate 1. Back Swing.

PURPOSE: To further strengthen the lower back.

POSITION: Lie on the floor on your stomach, legs straight and together, your arms close together and outstretched on the floor in front of you. Your head should be off the floor (neither forehead nor chin touching the floor).

ACTION: Slowly lift your right arm and left leg straight up from the floor. The arm should not twist or go out to the side, but should point straight ahead, close enough to your head to brush your ear. When you have lifted both limbs as high as you can, slowly lower. Repeat, lifting the left arm and right leg. Continue, rhythmically alternating legs and arms.

BREATHING: Breathe naturally; don't hold your breath.

REPETITIONS/GOAL: Since this exercise is somewhat more strenuous than the Alternate Leg Lift, you should begin with fewer repetitions. A good starting point would be 8 on each side, alternating; add 2 per side per week until you can do 15, 3 times a week.

Level III Maintenance Programme

The few exercises for maintenance on this Level are quite strenuous and should not be attempted by anyone who has not mastered all of the exercises on Level III at the maximum number of repetitions. Because they strengthen the entire pelvic area, these exercises are an excellent supplement to any other exercise regimen, from aerobics to yoga.

Level III Maintenance should be performed 3 times a week, except for the pelvic floor exercise which should be done daily. Also, as with maintenance at Level II, you should periodically test your pelvic fitness. Since you may become bored performing the same exercises indefinitely, alternate exercises are suggested for this level which you may substitute for the basic exercises from time to time.

Warm-ups:

Perform all warm-ups before exercising *every time* you work out (except for isometric workouts).

118

Abdomen

The exercise for maintenance of abdominal strength on Level III is the same as a basic exercise on that level: the V-sit, Abdominal Exercise 2.

To go to maintenance, continue to perform all of the exercises on Level III, reducing the frequency of workouts to 3 per week. When you get to the second abdominal exercise, the V-sit, add 2 repetitions per week until you have worked up to 15, performed with control and no sense of strain. At this point you may discontinue the other abdominal exercises except for periodic testing, which will be explained below.

Pelvic Floor

The maintenance exercise for the pelvic floor on all levels is 10 Slow Contractions, held for 6 seconds each, once a day. For supercontrol of the P-C, do 3 of these as P-C Isolations (Pelvic Floor Exercise 2, Level III).

Lower Back

The maintenance exercise for the lower back at Level III is identical with Level II Lower Back Exercise 4, the Alternate Leg Lift. This is because the similar exercise at Level III, the Back Curve, is too strenuous for multiple repetitions.

To go to maintenance, continue to perform all Level III exercises, reducing the frequency to 3 times a week. When you get to Lower Back Exercise 3, the Back Curve, substitute instead the Alternate Leg Lift. Begin with as many as you can do on each side, alternating; add 2 per side per week until you can do 30 per side. This is Level III maintenance.

Always follow this exercise with a recovery exercise such as the Cat Back (Lower Back Exercise 3, Level I).

Periodic Testing

Please see the note on the need for periodic testing at the end of the section on Level II Maintenance. Such periodic testing is as important for Level III as for Level II.

119

Summary of Level III Maintenance Programme

	REPETITIONS	FREQUENCY
Warm-ups	See Chapter 7	3 times a week
ABDOMEN		
V-sit	15	3 times a week
PELVIC FLOOR		
Slow Contractions	10	once a day
LOWER BACK		
Alternate Leg Lift	30 each side, alternating	3 times a week
Cat Back	3	3 times a week

To test your continuing pelvic fitness at Level III Maintenance, set aside a longer than usual exercise period one day every six weeks. During this exercise period, attempt to do each of the exercises in the Level III basic programme at the maximum number of repetitions. If you find any of the exercises difficult to do correctly at the suggested number of repetitions, return for a while to the basic Level III programme, performing all difficult exercises 3 times a week.

There is a sample chart provided on page 121 for you to keep track of your maintenance workouts, as well as the periodic testing programme every six weeks.

Level III Maintenance: Alternate Exercises

From time to time you may wish to substitute the following alternate exercises for the basic exercises in this maintenance programme. Not only will doing new exercises keep you from getting stale, it will exercise your muscles in slightly different ways.

After you have been on the Maintenance Programme for several weeks, and only after you have worked up to the maximum number of repetitions for maintenance, you may substitute the following either occasionally or for several weeks at a time (but always return to the basic exercises from time to time and make sure you can do them at the suggested number of repetitions).

MAINTENANCE RECORD LEVEL III

Exercise	Reps.	WEEK 1			WEEK 2			WEEK 3			WEEK 4			WEEK 5			WEEK 6			*
		Day 1	Day 2	Day 3	Day 1	Day 2	Day 3	Day 1	Day 2	Day 3	Day 1	Day 2	Day 3	Day 1	Day 2	Day 3	Day 1	Day 2	Day 3	
V-Sit	15																			
P-C Slow Contractions	10 daily																			
Alternate Leg Lift	30 ea. side																			
Cat Back	3																			

* Once every six weeks, test your pelvic fitness by performing all exercises in Level III at the maximum number of repetitions.

121

Abdomen

The following three exercises work all your stomach muscles; because they are somewhat less strenuous than the basic exercise, the V-sit, you will have to perform them at a greater number of repetitions to get the same effect.

Alternate 1. Roll-down and Roll-up (Abdominal Exercise 2, Level II). Perform exactly as instructed for Level II; begin with 15, 3 times a week, and add 2 per week until you can do 30.

Alternate 2. Chair Sit-up. The alternate bent-legged sit-up for the Level II Maintenance Programme (Abdominal Alternate 2), can also be used as maintenance for Level III. Again, simply increase the number of repetitions until you can do 30 of these sit-ups, 3 times a week.

Alternate 3. Scissors Swing. This exercise is also very strenuous, but may be more comfortable for some women who, because of their natural build, have a very bony tailbone and have a hard time doing sit-ups or V-sits without discomfort.

PURPOSE: To maintain abdominal strength, with special attention to the lower muscles.

POSITION: Lie on your back, arms spread at shoulder level, palms down.

ACTION: (1) Lift your right leg straight up toward the ceiling. Lower it and at the same time begin to raise your left leg up. Lower the left leg, bringing the right leg up again. Both of your legs should be in motion all the time. Be sure to bring both legs straight up as far as you can. Continue until each leg has been raised four times, then

(2) On the fifth swing, stop both legs together at a 45-degree angle and hold them there for a slow count of 3. Now continue the swing, and repeat (1) above, alternately bringing both legs straight up. Repeat. The sequence can be counted as follows: (swing) 1, 2, 3, 4; (rest) 1, 2, 3; (swing), 1, 2, 3, 4, etc.

BREATHING: Breathe naturally, in a rhythm with your leg swings.

REPETITIONS/GOAL: Begin with 4 repetitions of (1) and (2) (that is, 24 complete swings and 3 complete stops interspersed). Work up to 8 stops with 8 swings, which is maintenance level.

RECOVERY: Abdominal Rock (Abdominal Exercise 5, Level I).

TIPS: It is important to keep your lower back on the floor at all times during this exercise. If you have difficulty doing this or feel a strain, try modifying your position by lying on your back with your buttocks resting on the backs of your hands, palms on the floor. If the exercise is still too difficult, return to the Roll-up until your abdominal muscles are stronger.

Abdominal 'Supermaintenance'

Some women (and men) are so pleased with the visible results of doing sit-ups that they want to perform even more abdominal exercises for the firmness of their abdomen. While it is not necessary to go greatly beyond the strength goals in the Level III Maintenance Programme, you may wish to do so; this is particularly desirable if, for example, you play a sport such as tennis or squash in which trunk strength is very important, or if you run or walk long distances (because the backs of your legs and lower back will become so much stronger and tighter, relatively, than your abdominal muscles).

Move into a 'supermaintenance' programme only if you are in good health, free of any back problems, and experience no pain or strain when you do the regular maintenance programme.

Since the only way to increase a muscle's strength is to increase the work it must perform, many people continue to add to the number of sit-ups or V-sits that they do (sometimes working up to hundreds of these a day). An easier and less time-consuming way to increase your muscles' workload is to add a bit more weight to the part of your body that you are moving with your abdominal muscles.

The best way to do this is to hold a three- to five-pound weight while you do either a Roll-up or a Chair Sit-up. Begin in the suggested position, but instead of holding your hands behind your head, fold your arms across your chest and tuck your chin into your chest. Hold the weight in your hands just under the chin, and perform the exercise as instructed. Three to five pounds does not sound like much, but it will make a big difference in your ability to do the exercise, and will consequently increase your strength.

Lower Back

The best alternate exercise for the lower back is the same as the alternate for Level II, the Back Swing. Begin with as many as you can do, probably between 10 and 15, alternating; work up to 30 on each side.

*

123

All of the above exercises are challenging, but none should cause you any real difficulty if you have mastered all Level III exercises. If you are interested in improving your pelvic fitness beyond the point we have suggested, continue to perform *all* Level III exercises 3 times a week, concentrating on the P-C Isolation (Pelvic Floor Exercise 2) and the Pelvic Tilt (Pelvic Floor Exercise 3). For special situations and conditions, including improved sexual relations, see the exercises recommended in the chapters in Part III.

How to Stick with Exercise

There are probably as many 'good' excuses for skipping exercise as there are individual exercisers. Most of these excuses appear reasonable on the surface, but when examined they seldom stand up. In fact, creating an excuse often uses more energy than exercising in the first place.

Following are the excuses for skipping exercise that we have heard most often—and our answers, based on our own experience and that of hundreds of women who have successfully stuck to exercise programmes.

I don't have enough time to exercise.

For many women, this is a valid complaint, expecially when the exercise programme itself requires a good bit of time. For example, swimming at a health club involves going there, changing, swimming, showering afterwards, drying your hair, and going home. This excuse doesn't work on our programme, however.

Anyone can make time for anything she really wants to do. For example, Terry, an art consultant, has a hectic schedule that involves seeing new artists, attending gallery openings, and consulting with clients. 'I'd love to exercise but I just don't have time,' she says. Yet Terry always has perfectly manicured nails, and admits that it takes her forty-five minutes at least three times a week to apply and repair polish!

Often, making time for exercise means sacrificing time elsewhere —giving up the second cup of coffee over the newspaper, for example, or getting up ten minutes earlier. But the results of the exercise are so worthwhile and will make you feel so good that you won't miss the extra time.

For achieving pelvic fitness the total investment in time is truly minimal: counting everything, including the warm-ups and laying out your exercise mat, the entire routine will take no more than ten minutes, even at the very beginning when you are still getting used to the routines.

I'm too tired to exercise.

Again, this is sometimes a valid complaint. If you've just had a truly horrendous day with a crisis at the office, unexpected dinner guests, and you only got three hours' sleep last night because the baby was up with a stomachache, then perhaps today isn't the day to exercise, even though it's on your schedule.

In that case, go ahead and skip this one workout. You can make it up later from one of your two free days (or one of your four free days if you are on the maintenance programme). Otherwise, the excuse is empty. First, the effort involved in performing the routines is very small, and second, you will almost certainly feel much better and more refreshed after you have worked out. It is common for women enrolled in calisthenics or yoga classes (or in an aerobics programme) to report that no matter how tired they may have felt when starting, the workout itself was as refreshing as a nap.

It's too hot/cold to exercise.

This one scrapes the bottom of the barrel. If your city is in the grip of a major heat wave and you don't have a fan or air-conditioner and you usually schedule your workout for one in the afternoon, then it probably is too hot to exercise at that moment. The obvious solution is to change your daily workout to early morning or late afternoon when it's cooler—or to perform your workouts in front of a fan or in a room with an air-conditioner. It's hard to believe this advice is necessary, but many women approach exercise with such a negative attitude that they will not do anything to make themselves more comfortable.

If heat (or cold) is a problem for you, rather than blaming the weatherman, take a look at your own attitude toward exercise. Do you approach it with dread, as something to be rushed through? If that is the case, you probably don't take the time to make yourself as comfortable as possible during your workout. Try to remember that you are exercising as a gift to yourself, even though the actual workout may not be much fun.

The question of its being too cold to exercise is likewise just an excuse, because the act of exercising itself will serve to heat up your body, and you may even find it necessary to open a window to maintain comfort.

The moral of all this is that weather conditions change throughout the year, but your need for and benefits from exercise do not. You will not always be perfectly comfortable during a workout, but you are not always perfectly comfortable during *any* activity, from going shopping to attending the ballet. Just continue working out—and let the weather take care of itself.

I'm embarrassed for anyone to know I'm exercising.

This complaint is far more common among women who exercise than men. When the jogging boom began in the early seventies, far more middle-aged and older men than women participated at first, largely because the women were afraid to exhibit a less than perfect body. Further, many women were embarrassed to admit that they were exercising, lest someone think that they were jumping on the bandwagon of another fad.

This excuse is easily answered, however. First of all, since you are exercising in the privacy of your own home, no one outside your family need know that you have embarked on a programme to improve your pelvic fitness. Second, you needn't even exercise in front of your family—simply arrange your exercise schedule for a time when no one else will be around, or if that is impossible, try to find a little privacy in your bedroom.

Besides, the chances are that everyone in your family (and your friends) will be proud of you for taking the time to improve your physical condition, and may even help to keep up your interest with their feedback and enthusiasm.

I can't stay on an exercise programme now because we're going on vacation/guests are coming/the bedroom is being painted next month. . . .

Let's face it. There will always be something coming up in your life that can give you an excuse to stop working out. The trick is to keep going anyway. Of course, valid interruptions do arise from time to time, and you may have to postpone an occasional workout, but do try to make it up the next day or the day after that. If you promise yourself that you will *always* make up any skipped exercise session, you may find it easier simply to go ahead and devote that five minutes to your workout no matter what the interruption.

If your life is disrupted completely—by a move, for example, or a stay in the hospital—you may have to stop working out for a week or two. When things are back to normal, begin again as soon as you can, reducing the number of repetitions you are doing for each exercise until you get in the groove again.

As for vacations, they are a perfect time to exercise because you generally have fewer obligations when on holiday than at other times. Bring your progress chart along and do your routine in the privacy of your hotel room . . . or villa . . . or even on the beach. Since we usually tend to overindulge in rich foods on vacations, working out may be just what you need to salve your conscience and keep from getting too out of shape.

I can't stick with exercise because it is too boring.

Here we come to the main reason why more people don't exercise regularly. In fact, it is probably the underlying reason for all of the other excuses. The answer to this one may surprise you: the truth is that exercise is *not* boring. Boredom is almost always a reaction to some other feeling that is being covered up. Exercise by itself is a neutral activity which you 'make' boring by your approach to it.

It's true that exercise is not mentally stimulating, but it is not supposed to be; that is, the aim of exercise is not the same as that of reading a weighty philosophical tome or even a mystery novel. However, your mind can and should be occupied with trying to do the exercises correctly and, particularly for the isometric exercises, in visualizing the muscles working as they are meant to during the exercise.

It's also true that exercise is challenging and requires effort, but the only way a muscle can become stronger is for it to be challenged. It is not uncommon to be afraid of effort, that is, to dread the work that will be involved. In many cases that effort may be interpreted by your mind as boredom. Simply focusing your mind on what you are doing will usually help to banish this sort of boredom.

This is not to say that you will be entertained every time you work out; but you can reduce any sense of tedium by adopting a positive attitude and using your imagination. In fact, there are several strategies you can follow to assure that your exercise sessions, if not the most stimulating activity in the world, need never be boring.

A good first strategy is to listen to music while you work out, once you are familiar with the exercises (music may be too distracting while you are still trying to learn the routines). Turn on the radio or put on a favourite record; not only will music give you something pleasant to occupy your mind while you work out, but a good beat can help you to perform the exercises rhythmically and with more control.

If you aren't in the mood for music, and you can arrange an exercise space, another good solution is to watch TV while you work out. Game shows and the news are good for this kind of workout, because you needn't pay as close attention to them as you would to a drama.

Another strategy to keep from getting bored is to work out with a friend. While our programme takes so little time it's probably not worthwhile to meet someone every day, doing so occasionally can be a real boost. Furthermore, if you and your friend are both on the same programme, you can compare notes and encourage each other, thus making it more likely that neither of you will drop out.

On those days when you just can't face the thought of a workout, try reminding yourself of the progress you have made and the further progress you intend. If your stomach is flabby now, imagine it flat and firm; see your pelvic area becoming stronger and more flexible, your body more erect and graceful. You know from experience that you feel good psychologically and physically after you have finished a workout, so look forward to the end result.

Finally, to continue your programme indefinitely, don't let your-self get in a rut. Once the exercise habit is well established, you can start varying the times of your workouts if you want; if you always exercise in the morning, try an occasional evening workout for a change. On the maintenance programme, if your regular exercises become too routine, go back to the basic programme for a while or substitute the alternate exercises suggested in the maintenance programme.

Above all, try to look forward to exercise as something positive you are doing for yourself, and which you choose voluntarily to do.

I'm not making any progress.

This complaint is most common to women who have not had any experience with exercise in a long time. The sad truth is that the more out of shape you are, the longer it will take you to get back into good condition. This is only common sense—after all, if you were fifty pounds overweight you would not expect to lose that amount in two weeks—yet many women who are very out of shape may forget just how many years it has taken them to get that way.

This is not to say that it will take you as long to get back into shape as it took you to get out of it—fortunately, the body has amazing recuperative powers—but it will take a longer period of time the more out of condition (and overweight) you now are.

Still, no matter how out of shape you are now, you will begin to see some improvement in a very short time—from a few days to six weeks, depending on how regularly you perform the exercises. This progress is slow but *steady*; as long as you continue to exercise several times a week, you will improve in increments, and those increments will build until one day you will look back and realize what a long way you have come.

In the meantime, there are three ways you can prove to yourself that you *are* making progress.

The first is by far the most important, and that is to *keep a record of your workouts*. Sample progress charts for each programme and for maintenance are provided, and we recommend that you make several photocopies of the charts for each Level. That way you won't be tempted to skip a session because you don't have a fresh chart, or to stop recording altogether. Each time you work out, be sure to record the number of repetitions you are performing for each exercise so that you know when to add more repetitions. Also, having a visible record lets you look back over the days of exercise and see in black and white the progress you have made—it can give you a real sense of accomplishment to move from four repetitions of a challenging exercise to eight. Sometimes looking over your record can be just the psychological boost you need to do a given workout.

Recording your exercises every day will become a part of the habit of exercise and will help to reinforce that habit. Furthermore, keeping track of each session helps ensure that you won't skip one or two workouts during the week because you 'just can't remember.'

Although it is not absolutely necessary, it's a good idea to make a notation of how you felt when you worked out, and of any exercises that were especially difficult. This will alert you to the exercises to concentrate more on in future sessions. Also, and more important, these notations will give you an idea of your own energy cycles. Every woman who exercises or plays sports has days that are more or less difficult. In many cases, these follow predictable hormonal cycles; in every case you can be certain that some workout sessions will be very difficult and unpleasant, some will be easy and joyous, while many others will be neutral. If you record these fluctuations over a period of time, you won't get discouraged when you have one of those particularly difficult days (or weeks), because your record will demonstrate that these times are invariably followed by more pleasant workouts.

A second way to gauge your progress is to test yourself from time to time. Review the tests for pelvic fitness at the end of chapter 4. Without a doubt, you will perform better on them whether or not you think you are improving, as long as you continue exercising.

Finally, it is a curious fact that all of us tend to reach 'plateaus' in exercise and sports, during which further improvement seems slow or nonexistent. This is common to all forms of exercise, and while it is not completely understood, is widely recognized by physiologists. If you seem to reach such a plateau, it may be helpful to review the physiological information at the beginning of part II: this will reassure you that your muscles are continuing to become stronger although you may not see any visible progress for the moment.

I can't remember to do the isometric exercises.

There's no doubt that performing P-C contractions several times a day is a new and seemingly difficult experience for many women. But it should require conscious effort only for the first few days. In fact, the *more often* you perform the isometrics, the easier it will be to remember to do them. They will become almost automatic, something you do without thinking.

We have already suggested that you remind yourself to do your fast P-C contractions as soon as you wake up in the morning by programming yourself before you go to sleep. You should also do one set of your P-C, abdominal, and buttocks contractions while you are performing your daily workout. To remember to do the contractions at other times during the day, try taping strategic reminder notes where you are likely to see them: on the bathroom mirror, for example, or on the refrigerator.

Any of the basic contractions can be performed any time you are sitting or standing: while you are stirring a white sauce at the stove, for example, or while you are waiting in line at the post office. Furthermore, you can do more sets of contractions during the day than those recommended and will progress more quickly if you do so. Keeping this in mind may remind you to use otherwise idle moments, such as time spent in waiting rooms, to add another increment to your developing pelvic fitness.

A woman we know increased her fitness by the simple expedient of contracting her P-C muscle whenever she was waiting at a traffic light in her frequent short drives around town. She reported that she quickly became accustomed to performing the contractions while she was driving, and soon it became automatic to perform a set or two of contractions whenever she was out in her car.

The Nineteen Questions
Women Most Often Ask
About Our Programme

How can I be sure I'm doing the exercises correctly?

The most important step is to practise any new exercise very slowly for the first session or two without worrying about how many *times* you do it. If an exercise has more than one part, practise them separately before you combine them. Refer carefully to illustrations to make sure you are in the correct position for starting; in many cases performing an exercise in the wrong position will cause some of the benefits of that exercise to be lost. One of the best ways to make sure you are in the correct position is to perform in front of a full-length mirror, or ask a partner to check your position against the illustration.

Is it all right to do some of the exercises in the morning and the rest in the evening?

Our programme takes so little time that it should not be necessary to split it into two sessions; if on occasion you wish to do this, it would be all right, provided that you do warm-ups before each exercise session and that you follow the order presented for all exercises within a given group (for example, Abdominal Exercise 1 should always be followed by Abdominal Exercise 2).

Be sure to do all isometric exercises that require multiple repetitions several times during the day.

Some of the exercises are too hard for me and I can't do the minimum number of repetitions.

In most cases if you follow the order of the exercises, not moving to Level II before you have mastered the maximum number of repetitions for all Level I exercises, you should not have any difficulty performing all exercises at the suggested number of repetitions. However, if you have extreme difficulty with any one exercise—such as sit-ups, for example—start with as many as you can do and work up from there. Or, alternatively, perform half the exercises, rest for a few minutes, then perform the rest of the repetitions for that exercise. This is particularly helpful when you begin maintenance at levels II or III, since the suggested number of repetitions per exercise is much higher than for the basic programme.

Sometimes my muscles tremble when I perform the 'hold' part of an exercise. What does this mean?

Slight muscular trembling when performing exercise is perfectly normal, and simply means that your muscles are working harder than they are accustomed to. Continue to do the exercise, but don't further increase the number of repetitions until your muscles have become stronger.

I hate to do sit-ups. Can I skip that part of the workout?

For best results, our programme should be followed exactly as it is presented. If you hate sit-ups it is undoubtedly because your abdominal muscles are weak and flabby and you dread the effort of exercising them. Don't rush through your exercises—this will only make any discomfort more severe. Slow down and concentrate, especially when you perform any exercise that you find unpleasant. Remind yourself that with each sit-up your abdominal muscles are becoming stronger, and your tummy firmer and flatter.

When you have increased the strength of your abdominal muscles and begin a maintenance programme, it is all right to substitute another suggested abdominal exercise for sit-ups.

What if I have to stop exercising for a few weeks?

As we explained in the previous chapter, there is usually no reason to stop exercising altogether. However, if a hiatus of a few weeks is unavoidable, simply return to your exercise regimen as soon as you can, and start either on a lower level or at a lower number of repetitions for the exercises at the Level you were on.

Should I exercise if I'm ill?

As a general rule if you're really ill, if you're running a fever or have some other serious symptoms, the best thing to do is just stay in bed—why put your body under extra stress? If, on the other hand, you're just feeling a bit under the weather, working out may very well perk you up psychologically and make you feel better. Remember to be on guard for excuses not to exercise—for many women a slight ailment, alas, too easily constitutes such an excuse.

Can I exercise during my period?

Until very recently, many girls were excused from physical education classes when they were menstruating on the theory that any exercise at this time might be too strenuous or even dangerous. Current research and the personal experience of tens of thousands of women athletes has shown that this old theory is nonsense—not only is there no harm in exercising during your period, there may be actual benefit in terms of relieving any discomfort you feel at the time. As for exercising while you are actually having cramps, only you know if you feel too sick to work out, but many women find that exercise itself helps to relieve discomfort.

For specific exercises for help in relieving premenstrual tension and cramps, see chapter 16.

Why does my lower back hurt when I do abdominal exercises?

This very common complaint usually results from the fact that we have weak abdominal muscles relative to our back muscles; since the muscles are interconnected, the back muscles become strained when we try to do more work than the abdominal muscles are prepared for. If you experience marked discomfort in your back while doing any form of leg lift, try the following: slow down and do the exercise in as controlled a manner as possible; go only part way—that is, do not move into the most extreme position for the exercise; make sure that the small of your back is not arched—if necessary, check with a finger to make sure that your lower back is flat on the floor when that position is called for; and finally, try cutting down the number of repetitions until your abdominal muscles are stronger.

Always follow any strenuous abdominal exercise with a recovery exercise for the abdomen, such as the Abdominal Rock (Abdominal Exercise 5, Level I).

I can't seem to isolate the separate abdominal (or P-C) muscles in the advanced isometric exercises.

There are three keys to learning to isolate the muscles in isometric contractions: imagination, concentration, and practice. When you first start to do the contractions, particularly if your muscles have been very out of shape, you may have trouble sensing a difference in feeling between the lower P-C and the upper. Simply continue to practise the series of contractions, closing your eyes if necessary and *visualizing* the muscles squeezing tight from the bottom to the top. It doesn't matter whether you feel this difference at first or not. If you continue to do this on a regular basis, you will gradually be able to sense a difference as you become more aware of the different parts of the muscle.

The same applies to the abdominal isolation contractions, but in this case you have the additional aid of your fingers, to use both as a concentration device and for feedback. Perhaps you can't consciously contract the different abdominal muscles at first, but by lightly touching your abdomen with your fingertips, you will be able to feel when the different muscles are moving, and this feedback will gradually give you more control.

The most important thing is to not give up—with determination and practice, any woman can learn to do these exercises.

Speaking of the contractions . . . I'm not sure I'm contracting my P-C muscle correctly.

Women who have a very weak or damaged P-C muscle may have more than usual difficulty in learning to contract it voluntarily. One way to tell if your P-C is contracting is to insert two fingers just inside your vagina and contract your urinary sphincter as if to hold back the flow of urine: you should feel a tightening inside the muscular walls of the vagina.

If you cannot feel a contraction, or have difficulty performing this check, by all means ask your gynaecologist to monitor your attempts until you are sure you know what a P-C contraction feels like. For women with severe damage to the P-C muscle, there are mechanical aids that may help in performing these exercises. Such aids must be prescribed by a gynaecologist; for further details see the appendix.

I have no problem contracting my P-C, but I find it impossible to do without also contracting my rectum and abdominal muscles.

This is another common complaint and nothing to worry about. The more you practise contractions, the more these problems will resolve themselves. As you continue to do contractions on a regular basis, you will discover that the P-C itself will become so much stronger that it can be contracted without involving the other muscles. This may happen literally overnight or it may be a gradual process, but in the meantime just continue to do the exercises.

I find it difficult to do isometric exercises and still breathe naturally without holding my breath. Can this be dangerous?

It is true that it can be dangerous to hold your breath when you are doing certain strenuous exercises, particularly if you have high blood pressure. However, there is no danger of any injury if you do so on this programme. But holding your breath will prevent you from gaining complete control over the muscles you are exercising. As you keep practising, continue to *try* to breathe naturally, even if you must let up a little on the contractions to do so. In time you will be able to perform the contractions with perfect control while breathing in and out normally.

It's hard for me to contract my P-C with my legs spread slightly apart. Is it all right to cross my legs?

Women with a very weak P-C muscle will find it easier to do the contractions with their legs crossed because in this position the thigh and abdominal muscles can 'assist' the P-C. If you must cross your legs at first in order to learn the *feeling* of a P-C contraction, that is all right; however, for best results you must learn to contract the muscle in isolation. As soon as you have learned what a P-C contraction is like, gradually spread your legs until they are comfortably apart while you practise. With time it will become easy for you to achieve a full contraction in this position.

I don't seem to be getting any results. I'm doing the contractions at least once or twice a day, but I don't always remember to do them as many times as you recommend.

To get the benefits from the P-C exercises it is *essential* that you perform a minimum of 200 contractions a day at first. A young woman beginning our programme reported after three months that she had no results, yet she admitted she was only contracting her P-C muscle 10 times, 3 times a day. When we pointed out how important it was for her to greatly increase the number of contractions, she decided to give it a try.

'For a while I was doing it every half hour,' she reports. 'I felt like a lunatic, but in less than three weeks there was a real difference.

137

From not even being sure I was contracting, suddenly I had real control over the different parts of the muscle.'

To help remember to do frequent contractions, follow the strategies we suggested at the end of the last chapter. If necessary, enlist the help of your husband or roommate to remind you at first. After you have been exercising so often for a week or two, it will become almost automatic. Furthermore, the stronger your P-C muscle becomes, the more full contractions you will be able to perform during each session, and the less frequently it will be necessary for you to do them.

Is it all right to exercise while I'm pregnant?

As we have stressed, pregnancy is not the time to begin any new exercise programme, although most experts agree that it is desirable to continue any exercise you have been doing for as long as you are comfortable and have your doctor's permission. In chapter 17 there are a number of special exercises suggested for the months of pregnancy, as well as recovery exercises for after the delivery.

ALWAYS get your doctor's advice in regard to exercise or any other unusual activity during pregnancy.

Can older women do the pelvic fitness programme?

Our programme is designed for women of all ages. Many of the exercises can be performed by any woman no matter how old or out of condition she is. In addition, chapters 18 and 19 describe special, less strenuous exercises for women approaching menopause and after.

What will happen if I quit exercising?

Many women are reluctant to begin an exercise programme for fear that, if they stop, the muscular fitness they have achieved will immediately 'turn to fat.'

Luckily, such an outcome is impossible. Muscle is one kind of tissue and fat is another, and the one can no more change into the other than lead can be transformed into gold.

When you stop an exercise programme—this or any other—the muscular fitness you have achieved gradually will fade away. Your firm abdomen and supple waist will slowly return to a condition of flab; your P-C muscle will gradually lose its tone and strength.

But why should you allow that to happen? Staying on the programme isn't hard and doesn't take that much time. As we have

138

mentioned, if you must stop exercising for a period of time, simply begin again as soon as you can, at a somewhat lower level than where you left off. But the longer you put off getting back into your routine, the more out of condition you will become and the harder it will be.

Will the Pelvic Fitness Programme help me to lose weight?

The only way to lose weight is to burn more calories than you take in. Because these exercises are not strenuous or prolonged, they do not burn a significant number of calories, so unless you diet at the same time you will not lose weight on this programme. However, as you increase the strength and tone of your abdominal and back muscles, you will undoubtedly *appear* slimmer, particularly in the waist and abdomen.

Experts are agreed that the fastest and easiest way to lose weight is to combine a nutritionally sound diet with *vigorous* sustained exercise (such as walking, running, or swimming). For more information on losing weight combined with exercise, see the appendix.

14

Creative Relaxation

'I love the way exercise makes me look,' says the red-haired artist. 'But to be perfectly honest, this is my favourite part of the class.' As she speaks, she is stretched out on an exercise mat, her firm body motionless, her face smooth and peaceful, as if she hadn't a care in the world.

'It's like a massage,' adds her neighbour, a young woman in her early twenties. 'Afterwards you feel terrific all over.'

These women and a dozen others have just completed the final part of one of Maria's exercise classes: creative relaxation. Just as muscles must be trained to be strong, they must also, in many cases, be trained to relax.

It's no secret that our world is full of a number of stresses, from the harried, busy way we live to the daily doses of national and international news. For women who work and raise families as well, these stresses are compounded. Even happy events, such as a wedding, a new job, a dinner party, are now known to add to the toll of daily stress.

Stress can cause many unhealthy changes in our bodies—among them muscular tension, which pulls even strong, well-aligned muscles into unnatural positions. The resulting unconscious inner clenching can cause aches and pains which become, in their turn, yet another form of stress.

You can't avoid stress, but one of the best ways you can cope with it, in addition to exercising regularly, is to learn to totally relax your body. The benefits of total relaxation are many: if you set aside a few minutes a day just for relaxation, you will feel as rested as if you had taken a nap. You will find tension—mental and physical—melting away. It will be easier to sleep at night and, conversely, while you're awake and going about your business, your mind will be more alert.

Relaxation is also an important tool in coping with difficult life changes, such as pregnancy and menopause.

Yet many of us don't really know *how* to relax. It's not just a matter of sitting down and putting your feet up, *but rather of learning how it feels to let your muscles go, one by one.*

Relaxation Exercises

1. Deep Abdominal Breathing

If you stop and think about your breathing, you realize that your lungs expand to fill with air. However, the most important muscle used in breathing is actually the diaphragm, a tough muscle that divides your chest cavity from your abdomen. When you breathe in fully, your diaphragm drops down and your abdomen moves slightly out. Most of us have a tendency to breathe shallowly, moving our chests as the lungs take in a small amount of air and not allowing the diaphragm to fully expand.

Consciously forcing your abdomen out when you inhale pulls the diaphragm further down into the abdominal cavity and enables your lungs to fill more fully. This technique is sometimes known as 'belly breathing.' Consciously pushing your abdomen in as tightly as you can, conversely, will help to expel stale air from deep within your lungs. To practise belly breathing, get in a comfortable position, lying or sitting, and place your fingertips on your belly for feedback. Push your abdomen out, at the same time inhaling very slowly, taking in as much air as you can. Hold your breath a moment, then force your abdomen flat as you slowly exhale. Any time you are feeling tense, pressured, or upset, four or more complete belly breaths will help to calm your nerves and clear your mind. If you start to feel dizzy while practising deep breathing, hold your breath for the count of 6.

The following two techniques will enable you to achieve total muscular relaxation. Once you have learned how to do them you will be able to relax at will, any time, simply by making a mental inventory of the muscles in your body.

The best way to learn these exercises is to read the instructions slowly into a cassette or tape recorder, and play it back while you practise the techniques. Pause for 5 seconds after every sentence.

When you see ellipsis points (. . .) pause for 10 seconds before you continue reading.

If you do not have a recorder, simply read through the instructions several times until you are familiar with them. It is not necessary to follow them to the letter, and it's all right to check with the instructions as you practise. After you have practised the techniques a few times you will be able to do them from memory. For best results, bear the following in mind:

(1) Do the exercises when you have at least 5 minutes (better, 10 to 20 minutes), when you will not be disturbed. If possible, do them in a room with a comfortable temperature, lying on a firm surface.

(2) When the instructions call for a deep inhalation or exhalation, it means to do 'belly breathing' as explained above. Otherwise breathe naturally and don't hold your breath at any time.

(3) If the instructions ask you to visualize a favourite place or a restful scene, throw your imagination into it and really create the place in your mind, with all its sights, sounds, and sensations.

(4) Finally and perhaps most important, as you continue in the relaxation exercise, do frequent mental checks to make sure that you are not unconsciously tensing muscles anywhere in your body. The most common points of unnoticed tension are the shoulders, upper back, neck, back of the head, jaw, and forehead.

2. Deep Muscular Relaxation

Do this exercise at bedtime, at the end of a workout, or any time you need a break and will not be disturbed for at least 10 minutes.

Lie on your back on a comfortable, firm surface, and turn the lights low. Close your eyes. If you will not be using a tape, remember that the relaxation moves from the lower part of the body toward the upper part and from the extremities to the centre.

Imagine for a moment that you are at your favourite place. Look it over in your imagination. Gently roll your head left to right, massaging the back of your skull. Take a deep breath, then exhale completely. Again, inhale and exhale.

Now focus your attention on your right foot. Contract all the muscles of the foot, pointing the toe. Hold tightly, then relax. Turn back the toes of the right foot, pointing them toward your head. Hold, then relax.

143

Contract the muscles of your left foot. Point the toes, hold tight, and slowly relax. Turn the toes back, holding the tension, and slowly relax.

Contract all levels of your P-C muscle now, as tightly as you can. Hold, then slowly let it go.

Now, pinch your buttocks tightly together. Hold the muscles tight . . . then let them go.

Now concentrate on the abdominal area: pull your stomach in at the bottom, the centre, and the top. Hold tight; now relax first the bottom, then the centre, and then the top.

Now tightly squeeze your shoulder blades together. Hold, then let go. Pull your shoulders up toward the ceiling, hold and relax. Now shrug your shoulders, pulling them up as if to touch your ears. Let your chin drop, still holding your shoulders tight, then relax. Press your shoulders down toward your ankles, hold, and let go.

Now contract your chest muscles. Hold, and let go.

Now inhale deeply and exhale. Again inhale, then resume breathing normally.

Your arms are at the side of your body, palms down. Make a fist with your right hand. Keeping your arm on the floor, raise your fist. Hold it high, feeling the tension in your arm. Hold, then slowly lower the hand and relax. Bend the right arm at the elbow, tense all the muscles, hold, then relax. Now force your right arm against the floor, again creating tension in all the arm muscles. Hold tight, then completely relax the arm.

Now concentrate on the left arm. Palms down, make a fist with your left hand. Holding the arm down on the floor, raise the fist. Feel the tension in your arm, hold it tight, then slowly let it go. Bend the left arm at the elbow, contracting the muscles, creating tension in the whole arm. Hold tight, then let it go. Force your left arm against the floor. Hold, then relax.

Now focus your attention on the skull. Gently press your head against the floor, creating tension, then relax. Lift your head off the floor until your chin is touching your chest. Press and hold; then slowly relax.

Now make a big happy smile. Imagine you have just heard a wonderful joke. Hold the smile, tensing all your face muscles, then relax. Squeeze your eyes tightly shut, hold, and relax. Lift your eyebrows high up, creating tension in the forehead and the skull. Relax.

Inhale deeply, then slowly exhale, all the way out. Again inhale, then resume breathing normally.

Focus your attention on your feet. Both feet are becoming very heavy, warm, and relaxed. Feel the heaviness spread up to your ankles, your calves, to your knees and thighs. Now forget about both of your legs.

Feel the warm, heavy relaxation spread to your whole pelvic area, then up to your abdomen, your midriff, and your chest.

Focus your attention on your tailbone. Imagine the feeling of relaxation moving up each vertebra, one by one. Feel the tension disappearing from the middle part of your trunk as your spine seems to sink into the floor. Your shoulders are loose and relaxed. The back of your neck is relaxed. Your spine is touching the floor from the tailbone to the neck. Your trunk has become so warm and heavy you cannot move.

Now concentrate on both your hands. Feel them becoming heavy and warm. This feeling flows up your wrists to the lower arms and then the upper arms. Your whole body is so relaxed now it seems to fade away.

Now concentrate on your scalp. Imagine that it is a piece of wrinkled cloth—smooth it out. As your scalp relaxes you have a tingling feeling all over your head. Concentrate on your forehead. The muscles between your eyebrows are loose and relaxed. All tension is gone from your forehead. You feel a warm flow of relaxation on your scalp and forehead. Relax your eyes and all your face muscles. Make your face pliable. Drop your chin and let your head sink into the floor. Your eyeballs sink deep into your head and your tongue is at the back of your throat.

Now, fully concentrate on your breath. As you inhale, feel cool air in your nostrils. As you exhale, feel the warm air flowing out. Now observe the rhythm of your breathing. As you go into deeper and deeper relaxation your breathing will become very shallow and light. Now concentrate on your heartbeat. Feel the rhythm of your heart.

Imagine that you are lying on the beach, feeling warm sand under your body, feeling the warm sunshine on your face, and hearing the soothing sound of the waves. Imagine you are watching the waves roll in and out. Now synchronize your breathing with the movements of the waves . . . inhale as the waves roll in . . . exhale as the waves roll out. Imagine that you have become one with the ocean as you breathe. Gently inhale and exhale. Inhale . . . exhale.

Continue until you are completely rested. When you want to come out of relaxation, first move your fingers and toes gently and slowly. Take a deep breath and exhale completely. Again inhale deeply, filling your body all the way up with air. Then exhale all the way to the bottom of your stomach. Again take a deep breath and lift your arms over your head, stretching from your fingertips to your toes, then exhale and pull your knees up to your chest. Lift your head up toward your knees, roll gently left to right, massaging the small of your back. Then roll forward and backward and come up to sitting position.

Inhale deeply, stretch both arms over your head, reaching for the ceiling, lower them, and open your eyes.

3. Differential Relaxation

This is a more advanced relaxation technique, which should be practised only after you have mastered deep relaxation. Again, you will get best results if you first read the instructions into a tape recorder and then play the tape. If you cannot do this, read over the instructions several times and practise them.

In addition to providing you with deep and restful relaxation, this exercise will help you to learn the difference between tension and relaxation. For that reason it is an especially good exercise for women who plan to have natural childbirth, where part of the goal is to learn to relax the rest of your body (especially the P-C) while only your uterus is contracting.

First, lie down and close your eyes. Running quickly through the first part of the Deep Muscular Relaxation, inventory your body to make sure all muscles are relaxed from your toes to the top of your head.

Now concentrate on your right arm. Pull all the muscles tight from your fist to your upper arm. While you are holding tight, have a sense that the rest of your body is relaxed. Compare the right arm with the left arm. Feel the difference between tension and relaxation. Breathing naturally, relax your right arm.

Now concentrate on the left arm. Tense all the muscles of the hand and arm. Hold the tension there while keeping the rest of your body relaxed. Check your scalp, forehead, neck, lower back, and leg muscles. All should be relaxed. Compare the right arm with the left. Hold the tension, then release.

Now concentrate on your right arm and left leg. Pull all the muscles tight, from foot to thigh and hand to upper arm. The opposing limbs should be loose and relaxed. Compare the tense limbs with those that are relaxed, then let all tension go from your arm and leg and rest a moment, all muscles relaxed.

Now focus your attention on your left arm and right leg. Pull all the muscles tight. Check the rest of your body. If you find tension anywhere, release it. Again, compare the opposing limbs. Note how it feels to be relaxed and how it feels to be tense. Relax the limbs and rest a moment.

Now contract your P-C muscle, keeping your abdomen, buttocks, and thighs relaxed. Compare the feeling of tension in your P-C with the relaxation in the rest of your pelvic area, then let it go.

(Do not do this part if you have back problems.) Slightly arch the back, creating tension in the lower back. Hold, breathing normally, then let the tension go.

Pull your abdomen in. Hold your stomach muscles tight, pressing your lower back against the floor, while keeping the rest of your body relaxed. Hold, then release.

Concentrate on your shoulders. Shrug your shoulders, pulling them up as far as they will go. Hold tight. You may feel some discomfort at the back of your neck, but the rest of your body should remain relaxed. Hold, then let go.

Now concentrate on your scalp. Gently push your head against the floor, creating tension in the back of your neck and scalp. Hold, then relax the neck and scalp. Lift your head off the floor, bringing your chin to your chest. Stretch the back of your neck, holding tension in the front of your neck. Slowly relax.

Roll your eyebrows up, tightening your forehead. Hold, then relax.

Now inventory your entire body from the soles of your feet to the top of your head. If you find tension anywhere, notice it and release it. Your entire body is now relaxed.

If you want to continue, lie there and enjoy deep relaxation. If you are ready to come out, gently move your fingers and toes, take a deep breath, exhale completely, and again inhale.

On the next inhalation swing your arms up over your head and stretch from head to toe. Relax, let your body go limp, and when you are ready, open your eyes and sit up.

Part Three

———————

**Lifelong
Pelvic
Fitness**

CHAPTER

15

Pelvic Fitness in Childhood

In this chapter and the rest of the book we will look at ways in which pelvic fitness can help to cure or prevent specific problems that women may meet as a matter of course as they mature and grow older. Just as our needs for food change throughout life, so do our exercise needs, although the basic pelvic fitness programme can and should be followed indefinitely.

Most of the exercises that follow will be variations on exercises you have already learned. Any completely new exercise will, of course, be fully explained. The remaining chapters can be thought of as a lifelong guide that will give you maximum control over the fitness, health, and well-being of your changing woman's body.

Childhood

Sara W., a middle-aged mother of five, remembers that as a child, 'I couldn't help wetting the bed in the middle of the night. This problem lasted until I was a teenager, and nothing seemed to help. I tried everything—no water after 5:00 P.M., even setting an alarm before I went to bed. My parents took it in stride, but it was terribly embarrassing, and I never spent the night with friends the way other girls did.'

Sara's problem disappeared by the time she reached high school, but after the birth of her third child, in her mid-thirties, she began to suffer from stress incontinence, or involuntary leakage of urine. Luckily, she enrolled in an exercise class in which P-C control was taught, and the problem disappeared. Today Sara believes, 'If I had only known about those exercises when I was a little girl, I'm sure I would never have had the problem in the first place.'

Many experts would agree with her. Dr. J. P. Greenhill, an expert on exercise for treatment of pelvic disorders, writes that the majority of women he has treated for P-C muscle weakness had evidence of these problems developing as a child. The first signs were usually slowness to learn urinary control and/or a continuing problem with bed-wetting. Other signs included a 'vague feeling of pelvic discomfort,' similar to the sort of congestive discomfort many women experience just prior to their menstrual periods.

The probable cause of these difficulties is improper use of the P-C from the time of toilet training onward. As we saw in chapter 3, this occurs because the nerves that control the P-C do not develop fully until the second year of life. If toilet training takes place too early or if there is a lag in normal development, the P-C may be helped to do its job by the abdominal and inner thigh muscles, and thus never develop full strength or control.

Misuse of the P-C in childhood can contribute to many problems later in life. In addition to those we have discussed, these include recurrent bladder problems and difficulty in sexual relations, as well as difficult deliveries and injury during childbirth. The irony is that most of the problems that appear in midlife are often attributed solely to injuries suffered during childbirth, when the cause actually is lifelong incorrect use of a muscle.

Dr. Greenhill feels that pelvic exercises should be performed throughout a woman's life, starting in childhood. Furthermore, he believes that these exercises should be included as an 'essential part of teenage sex education,' and at the very least be taught routinely as part of the premarital examination. A woman exercise instructor who agrees adds, 'If these simple exercises could be taught to girls in school, so much suffering could be avoided.'

Since P-C exercises are seldom taught even to grown women who are already suffering from the effects of a weak P-C, it seems unlikely that this utopian hope will be realized any time soon. Furthermore, because the P-C muscle is associated with what some people still believe to be a taboo area of the body, it is unlikely that school boards across the country will rush to approve a system of pelvic exercises for impressionable youngsters.

Therefore, it is up to you as a mother, aunt, or older friend to impart this information to young girls whom you care about. Luckily, the basic P-C contraction, once taught, can be practised by the child without supervision.

Menstruation

The many myths about menstruation found in the folklore of all cultures as well as in modern scientific writing are beginning to vanish: no longer is it believed, for example, that a menstruating woman will cause cattle to sicken and die if she looks at them. Changing too is the myth that any distress a woman experiences at this time is all in her head; doctors are finally beginning to recognize that there are a variety of causes—chemical, hormonal, anatomical —for such disorders as premenstrual tension and dysmenorrhea (cramps).

Unfortunately, researchers are not yet agreed on the nature or mechanism of these causes, and many of the best popular books on the subject of women's health still contradict one another. On one point, however, they are all agreed: while menstrual disorders cannot really be cured, any discomfort both before and during a period can be greatly lessened through a variety of means, one of the most important of which is exercise.

Menstrual disorders that can be eased by exercise fall into two categories: premenstrual syndrome and cramps. Premenstrual syndrome is most common in women over twenty-five, and usually begins up to a week before the period. It includes such physical symptoms as painful breasts, headache, congestion in the pelvis, weight gain, aching legs and feet, and psychological feelings of irritability and depression. In some women premenstrual syndrome lasts so long and is so disruptive that they can begin to feel, as one thirty-two-year-old woman puts it, 'As if I'm always either premenstrual or menstrual.'

The symptoms of premenstrual syndrome are thought to be caused (or exacerbated) by increased hormone levels, with consequent retention of fluid in the body. (Interestingly, a recent study at the University of Maryland School of Medicine found that women whose mothers prepared them for menstruation in a positive way reported far less tension and fewer symptoms of premenstrual syndrome than did those young women whose mothers taught them to approach the menses with dread.)

The second type of menstrual disorder that is often relieved by exercise is cramping, or pain during the menstrual period. There are two types of cramping: primary, which occurs mainly in young women just beginning their periods, and secondary, which most commonly appears in women over thirty, and which is frequently associated with premenstrual syndrome.

For all practical purposes, however, the two types of cramps are the same—they hurt.

The Value of Exercise for Premenstrual Syndrome

'I used to be a real witch before my period,' reports a thirty-six-year-old teacher. 'And then I started jogging every day. I don't know what it did—but even though my breasts still hurt sometimes, I never get in those rotten moods I used to.'

This young woman, who has gone on to become a very good road racer, discovered by accident what many women are now hearing from their doctors: that regular, *vigorous* exercise can help to prevent or alleviate premenstrual syndrome. Why it does so is not completely understood; theories include the possibility that, since this condition is caused at least in part by congestion of the pelvic area, exercise, by improving blood circulation, may help to break up that congestion.

If you have a tendency to get premenstrual tension, by all means begin to increase the level of your activity for a week or so prior to your period. Swim, jog, play tennis, and/or walk whenever possible. While it is true that you may not feel as energetic now as at other times, you undoubtedly need the exercise more. Performing the pelvic fitness exercises more often may help too, by increasing blood flow to the pelvic area and thus easing the congestion.

Poor posture, too, is blamed for some of the problems of premenstrual syndrome as well as for some of the common symptoms of discomfort in pregnancy. Dr. Arthur A. Michele, author of *Orthotherapy*, recommends exercises to increase the flexibility of the entire pelvic area and especially to improve the posture. For more information on posture exercises, see chapter 18.

154

Cramps

For many women, particularly those who have been told that cramps are psychosomatic, this condition can be very distressing and depressing. Most women who suffer from cramps have worked out their own home remedies—ranging from a couple of aspirins to a stiff belt of scotch. Another tried and true help is curling up with a heating pad.

We have already pointed out that you are less likely to suffer from severe cramping or premenstrual tension if you are accustomed to getting regular exercise. What is surprising is that doing certain exercises *while* you are having cramps is sometimes just as effective as taking a pain-killer.

'I've only had my cramps completely *cured* twice in my life,' reports a thirty-year-old magazine editor. 'Once it happened when I went to a chiropractor for something else, and the other was the time I had a date to go bicycling in the country and just couldn't give it up. Once my legs started pumping, all the discomfort just vanished and never came back.'

Exercises seem to relieve cramping in several ways. Bicycling, as in the example above, probably works by increasing blood flow and helping to break up pelvic congestion. Other exercises may help by shifting the position of the pelvic organs and relieving tension in the area. Try some or all of the following exercises the next time you experience cramps. You needn't do them all or in any particular order. Simply experiment until you find the exercise or exercises that work best for you.

P-C Contractions

For some reason, possibly because rapidly contracting the pelvic floor increases blood flow, a series of rapid, full P-C contractions can sometimes help to stop or lessen cramps. Also, a strong contraction at the moment of a very severe cramp can help to lessen its severity.

THE BOW

This yoga exercise has been found by many women to help lessen or banish cramps. Why it should do so is not known; perhaps, as one gynaecologist speculates, it shifts the position of the uterus, relieving abdominal pressure.

POSITION: Lie on your stomach with your chin resting on the floor. You should be as relaxed as possible.

ACTION: (1) Bend your legs and bring your feet up as close to your back as you can. Reach behind and grasp your feet with both hands.

(2) Now lift your knees and your upper trunk from the floor as far as you can. Hold for a few moments, then slowly return to starting position.

BREATHING: Breathe naturally.

REPETITIONS: 1 or 2 times.

TIPS: If you find this very difficult, don't worry about it; simply holding your feet as in step (1) will help to stretch your lower pelvic area and relieve discomfort.

Back Slant (Lower Back Exercise 4, Level III)

This exercise is extremely effective in relieving cramps, particularly when they are accompanied by low backache.

Since the Back Slant is a recovery exercise and not at all strenuous, it can be performed by any woman, no matter what level of the pelvic fitness programme she has reached.

Table Stretch

POSITION: Kneel down on your hands and knees, your back straight and parallel to the floor. Relax your head and let it drop forward.

ACTION: (1) Slowly and gently pull your right leg up toward your chest, then extend it straight out to the back. Repeat, in a gentle swinging motion. Repeat with the left leg.

BREATHING: Exhale when you pull the knee toward your chest, inhale as you extend it.

REPETITIONS: 8 on each side. Repeat if necessary for relief.

Deep Abdominal Breathing (Relaxation Exercise 1)

This exercise, which is given in chapter 14, can sometimes help with cramps. Lie on your back with your fingertips lightly resting on top of your abdomen, and do at least 20 full 'belly breaths.' Stop if you become light-headed and hold your breath for at least 6 seconds before continuing.

Rapid Breathing

This is another yoga exercise. If it is new to you, practise it *before* you are actually suffering distress.

POSITION: You may do this in any position you find comfortable, standing or sitting.

ACTION: (1) Strongly contract your abdominal muscles (all of them). At the same time exhale fully.

(2) Quickly relax the stomach muscles; you will automatically inhale.

(3) Immediately contract and strongly exhale again. Repeat all steps.

REPETITIONS: Up to 20 rapid breaths; more than this may cause light-headedness.

TIPS: The speed of these contractions is just a fraction of a second, and because of the explosive nature of the breaths you will sound as if you are 'huffing and puffing.' If you find yourself beoming light-headed, hold your breath for a count of 6 before continuing. This exercise can also be done in slow motion, and is just as effective. It is better to practise the fast contractions first, however, because they are easier to learn.

Pelvic Tilt II

POSITION: Lie on your back, bending both your knees, your arms at your sides.

ACTION: (1) Inhale, at the same time arching your back so that there is a small space between your lower back and the floor.

(2) Exhale, forcing your lower spine flat against the floor. At the same time raise your head and your knees, bringing your feet up off the floor. Your head and knees should come close to meeting.

(3) Return to start.

BREATHING: See above.

REPETITIONS: 2 or 3 complete movements.

TIPS: You should feel a stretching in the lower back. Do this exercise *very* gently; do not force it.

Remember—if you continue to practise the Pelvic Fitness Programme, you are far less likely to have severe menstrual problems.

The Childbearing Years

Birth Control

Probably no other single function so affects a woman throughout her life as her fertility and the possibility of becoming pregnant. Women who do not want to have children must constantly be aware of their own cycles if they are sexually active; although most men today are happy to cooperate, the ultimate responsibility always falls on us.

Unfortunately, we cannot give you an exercise that will prevent conception. However, the state of your pelvic fitness can have a direct bearing on birth control in several ways. This is especially true if you use the diaphragm, which is growing in popularity as horror stories about the Pill and the IUD continue to surface. As you probably know, the diaphragm is a thin disk of rubber surrounded by a coiled circular rim, which is held in place by the anatomy and musculature of the vaginal canal. There is some evidence that women with very poor P-C muscle tone are unable to hold the diaphragm in place correctly, thus greatly reducing its effectiveness. For this reason it is especially important to do daily P-C contractions if you rely on this method of birth control.

In addition, as we mentioned earlier in the book, the condition of your P-C muscle can affect the size diaphragm you wear. For maximum protection it is important to wear a diaphragm that fits exactly. One of the authors of this book found that after a few months of doing the Pelvic Fitness Programme her P-C tone had so increased that she needed a new diaphragm size.

Exercise has no known effect on the other common methods of birth control. However, the more fit your pelvic muscles, the less likely you are to suffer unpleasant side effects if you use the Pill or an IUD.

Infertility

It is a tragedy of our time that many couples who want to have children are unable to. For poorly understood reasons, possibly related to widespread use of the Pill, this problem seems to be growing.

In spite of a large number of sophisticated medical tests, in many cases the cause of infertility remains unknown. Although there is as yet no scientific proof, it is possible that exercise may help in some cases. For several years, Maria has been teaching exercises to women in an experimental infertility programme. Many of these women subsequently have been able to conceive, have normal pregnancies, and bear healthy babies at term.

Gena, twenty-eight years old, had been to several doctors, who could find nothing wrong with either her or her husband. 'They told me I was nervous, which I already knew. But there was no advice they could give me but to wait and take more tests.' On Maria's advice she began to do exercises for general fitness and pelvic health.

'For the first time I felt I actually was affecting my body,' she says. 'And finally, after eight months, I became pregnant.' Today the mother of an active nine-month-old son, Gena advises other infertile women to try exercise. 'We have no idea if it was the exercising that finally caused me to conceive. But it gave me a lot of peace of mind. I felt so helpless before, as if it were out of my control.'

Gena's doctor felt the exercises at least helped her psychologically; beyond that little is known about the relationship between fertility and fitness. Apart from the psychological aspects, however, there's no doubt that a high level of fitness allows all body systems to function at their best.

Another possibility is that the exercises specifically for the pelvic floor and associated muscles may improve fertility by helping to bring all organs into better alignment.

Furthermore, since in order for the sperm to fertilize the egg in the first place it must enter the uterus, a strong, muscular P-C muscle may be able to help propel the sperm to the cervical opening. Whether or not exercises aid conception in this way is still undetermined, but many of the women who have tried exercise are convinced that it was the deciding factor in enabling them to conceive.

If you suffer from infertility you should, of course, consult a doctor, and both you and your mate should be tested to see if a physical cause of the problem can be found. In the meantime, however, and even if a cause is found, you have nothing to lose and everything to gain by trying the routine that follows.

Pelvic Fitness Programme for Infertility

The most important thing you can do if you are trying to become pregnant is to get yourself into the best overall physical shape possible. Not only will this probably maximize the chances of conception, it will make any subsequent pregnancy and delivery safer and easier. We recommend the following regimen for women who are having difficulty conceiving.

1. Begin an aerobics programme for total physical fitness. Your basic exercise, which you should do at least four times a week, can be jogging, walking, swimming, cycling, aerobic dancing, jumping rope, or a combination of these exercises. See the appendix for more information on aerobics.

2. Follow the programmes for pelvic fitness presented in this book. Although it is not absolutely necessary to progress to Level III, it is recommended; in any case, practise until you are able to do the maximum repetitions of all exercises at Level II. Note carefully which exercises are most difficult for you and concentrate on those.

3. At least twice a day spend one to several minutes in the reverse pose described below. Do not attempt this if you have high blood pressure or back trouble—instead, lie on a slant board for five to ten minutes.

Half Shoulder Stand

PURPOSE: To reverse the flow of blood and tone the pelvic area; to allow all organs to return to their natural position; to relax the legs and lower part of the body. *Do not perform this exercise if you have high blood pressure.*
POSITION: Lie on your back, your arms at your sides.

ACTION: (1) Pull both knees to your chest and gently rock yourself up and down.

(2) Holding your hips firmly with your hands and keeping your upper arms on the floor, roll your body up so that your feet and derriere are pointing into the air. Your knees should be above your face. If it is comfortable for you, straighten your legs at an angle over your head.

(3) Wiggle your toes and make circles with your ankles. Stay in this position for the count of 30, or longer if you are comfortable.

(4) Slowly roll your back down to the floor and lower your legs, keeping your head and upper back on the floor. Rest a moment, then

(5) Pull your heels close to your buttocks and raise your buttocks as high as you can, keeping your back straight. Hold for a count of 4, then lower your body and relax.

BREATHING: Breathe naturally; do not hold your breath.

REPETITIONS/GOAL: Do once; start by holding the extreme position for 30 seconds and work up to 1 minute or more.

TIPS: Do not strain or force at any time when performing this exercise. Keep your neck, shoulders, and back of the head in contact with the floor and relaxed at all times.

4. Relaxation. It has been found in most infertility studies that women who try to conceive without success are generally tense and anxious; techniques to promote relaxation, such as meditation, have been very helpful to some. In addition or instead, perform one of the relaxation exercises described in chapter 14 once a day.

Apart from the knowledge that you are doing something active to help the problem, pelvic fitness can decrease the anxiety associated with a common technique for increasing fertility. To assure that the sperm have a maximum chance of entering the cervix, infertile women are often advised to elevate their feet after lovemaking for a period of up to twenty minutes. This can be uncomfortable, and for many women is an added source of stress. Once you have achieved very good vaginal tone, your doctor may agree that assuming this extreme position is no longer necessary (although you should stay in bed and refrain from washing yourself for at least twenty minutes).

Pregnancy

There is probably no other time in a woman's life when fitness is so important as during the months of pregnancy. Unfortunately, pregnancy itself is the *worst* time to begin a fitness programme. The best time to get into shape is *before* you become pregnant. We urge any woman who is thinking of conceiving to prepare for this event for at least several months beforehand. The results, in terms of your own health and well-being, as well as that of the child, will be more than worth it.

Exercises to Do before You Get Pregnant

The exercise programme recommended for women who are trying to conceive can be followed by women of any degree of fertility who are considering pregnancy. In addition to building to the highest fitness level you can in the basic Pelvic Fitness Programme, concentrate on

1. Overall, aerobic fitness.

Aerobics are the best exercises for improving your stamina. If you build up to a good level of aerobic fitness before you become pregnant, with your doctor's permission you will probably be able to continue your programme throughout much, if not all, of the pregnancy.

The importance of this sort of fitness in pregnancy cannot be emphasized too much. For example, a recent medical study revealed that *the average duration of labour* from the breaking of the bag of water to delivery *was twice as fast for trained athletes as for nonathletes*.

A skier, Trina Hosmer, who had begun jogging several years before it was fashionable, was a pioneer in this respect. She continued to run on the roads near her home throughout her pregnancy, despite 'some peculiar looks from drivers and near-accidents.' One day she went out for her four-mile daily run in spite of feeling 'a little queasy.' She thought the run would perk her up. It was toward the end of this run that she realized her queasiness was actually the beginning of labour pains. 'I barely had time to get home and change,' she reports. She entered the hospital at 4:00 P.M. and her first son was born fifty-two minutes later.

While aerobics programmes may appear to be time-consuming, almost any woman can work, say, half an hour of steady walking into her daily routine. For further information, see the appendix.

2. Pelvic fitness

Work up to the highest Level of the Pelvic Fitness Programme that you can. Pay particular attention to the strength of your lower back, which will bear a great deal of the stress of your pregnancy.

3. Breathing and relaxation

Perform one of the relaxation exercises in chapter 14 once a day.

During the Pregnancy

Leigh W., a mother of six now in her mid-thirties, remembers that when she became pregnant with her first child she had no idea what she was doing. 'The doctor told me he'd take care of everything, and I thought, "Oh, good."' Her doctor prescribed a good diet for her and told her to take it easy. On the matter of exercise and preparation for childbirth, however, he was silent, and the result was a long and difficult birth that resulted in the need for heavy anaesthesia, combined with a forceps delivery, which slowed Leigh's recovery.

'When I got pregnant the second time I was lucky enough to meet a woman who taught childbirth exercises,' Leigh says. 'I started going to classes and all the other births were easy. I never even needed pain-killers.'

If you are now pregnant, by all means enroll in a class teaching exercises and preparation for childbirth. Even if you or your doctor thinks that you will deliver your child with the help of medication, the preparation will be invaluable, teaching you to understand what is happening to your body through each stage of labour. If possible, attend with your husband or partner, who will help you practise the exercises.

In addition to exercises recommended in your class, the following programme will help you have a more comfortable pregnancy and labour, and return to shape more quickly.

1. If you are now doing an aerobics programme such as jogging, keep it up as long as your doctor permits (and this may very well be throughout your entire pregnancy). If you have not yet begun such a programme, now is not the time to start one. However, unless your doctor disagrees, you should make an effort to walk as much as you can, at least one half hour a day, to improve your circulation and build stamina.

164

2. Continue the exercises for pelvic fitness. If you are just now beginning, start with Level I and work up to the maximum number of repetitions for each exercise. This will make a real difference in terms of your overall pelvic fitness and, thus, in your response to labour, delivery, and recovery. When you have fully recovered from the birth, you can move on to a higher level of the programme.

3. Take good care of your back. Pregnancy makes incredible demands on your body. As the baby grows, the entire centre of gravity of your body shifts. Your posture will become very different as the natural curve of your back becomes exaggerated. The abdominal exercises you did before pregnancy (and during the early months) will help your back bear the unaccustomed load.

Whenever you can, relax your back, reversing the curve. Take frequent rest breaks, curling up on your side. If you are comfortable doing it, and your doctor agrees, perform the Cat Back (Lower Back Exercise 3, Level I) when you are feeling a strain.

Finally, avoid pushing or lifting heavy objects.

4. Do exercises for relaxation, as recommended in the section on infertility. See chapter 14 for specific exercises.

5. As you continue doing P-C contractions, begin to concentrate on learning to relax the P-C. This will be extremely important during delivery: as Elizabeth Noble points out in *Essential Exercises for the Childbearing Years,* a supple P-C muscle that can be relaxed is far less likely to tear during delivery, resulting in less of a need for episiotomy. (Although as she also points out, doctors often perform this incision as a matter of course in this country. If you have an episiotomy you will be able to rebuild the strength of the P-C much faster if it was in good shape and you knew how to exercise it in the first place.)

Special Exercise for Breech Birth

As knowledge about exercise for women grows, experts are finding that many conditions, once thought to be incurable or requiring surgical intervention, are often taken care of through simple exercises. The following exercise, first reported in *Ob-Gyn News* in 1977, is reported to turn breech births in a large number of

165

cases, thus avoiding a difficult instrument delivery or the increasingly common Caesarean section.

If your doctor suspects your baby will be born in breech position, ask his permission to try this exercise. To be effective, it must be performed twice daily for two or three weeks starting at the thirtieth week of pregnancy. Even when the technique does not turn the baby to a more normal presentation, it is said frequently to dislodge the baby from the abnormal presentation enough to make outside manipulation sufficient for delivery.

POSITION: Lie on a hard surface with your pelvis raised above your head by 9 to 12 inches with the aid of stacked pillows.

ACTION: Do not move; merely hold the position for 10 minutes.

WHEN TO PERFORM: Twice a day, on an empty stomach, before lunch and dinner.

After Delivery

One of the most common complaints of women who have borne children is the difficulty in getting their shape back after pregnancy. Who can forget that Scarlett O'Hara was so dismayed by her new matronly figure that she decided to forgo all sex rather than risk further waist and hip spread? If only someone had told Scarlett of the miracles of postpartum exercise, maybe she and Rhett would have stayed together.

In any case, the role of exercise in returning the body to its former shape cannot be overemphasized, 'I gained only ten pounds during each of my pregnancies,' says a forty-year-old mother of two. 'With exercise I was back to normal within a month after birth. My sister never exercised at all and by her third child she looked middle-aged.'

A shapely figure is not the only goal of postpartum exercise, of course; in fact, this work is essential for returning the badly stretched P-C to normal health. For quickest, maximal recovery, you should begin restorative exercises as soon as possible after delivery. By as soon as possible, we mean you should begin within hours after delivery, while still in bed. Of course you will not do anything strenuous, but it is extremely important to begin to reestablish the nerves and blood supply to exhausted and possibly damaged muscles.

Among the exercises that can be performed right away are P-C contractions and isometric contractions for the abdomen.

Elizabeth Noble points out that beginning this exercise may be quite discouraging at first, since the muscle can be so stretched that no matter how hard you try to contract it you will see no result. However, keep trying and you will eventually succeed.

Even women who have had an episiotomy can do P-C contractions. Since the contractions themselves bring the edges of the wound closer to each other, there is no danger of the stitches tearing (and besides, you will probably have such poor control over the muscle at first that it will barely move).

The abdominal exercises can be performed as you lie in bed. Do the contractions described in Level I of the Pelvic Fitness Programme, squeezing the muscles in order from the bottom to the top. This will quickly lead to fuller control of the muscles, as well as to a flat, prepregnant tummy.

The Pelvic Fitness Programme should, of course, be resumed as soon as you feel up to it and your doctor agrees. No matter what level you were on before, it would be wise to begin again on Level I, although you will undoubtedly progress very quickly, depending on how fit you were before delivery.

Special Conditions during the Childbearing Years

Although childbearing is one of the most natural functions in the world, there is no question that it puts a strain on your whole body. The following conditions, while they may appear at any age, and while they are not necessarily connected with childbearing, often appear for the first time or become worse during pregnancy. Each of these problems will, however, respond to exercise.

Backache, Sciatic Pain

As we mentioned earlier, the centre of gravity shifts during pregnancy, resulting in an exaggerated curve of the lower back, producing pain in many women. In addition, some women suffer from sciatic pain at this time—a sharp, spasmlike pain usually felt in the buttocks and sometimes radiating down the back of the leg all the way to the foot.

Although sciatic pain can occur at any time, it is especially common during pregnancy because the extra weight in the abdominal cavity compresses the sciatic nerve as it passes through the opening in the pelvis.

For general exercises for backache, see the next chapter. In addition, the following exercise should help to bring relief from sciatic pain.

BENT-LEGGED CROSS

POSITION: Lie on your back, your legs straight, your arms resting on the floor straight out at shoulder level.

ACTION: (1) Inhale, then as you exhale, bring your right knee as close to your chest as you can.

(2) Lower the bent right leg across your body to the left side, as far as possible, keeping your upper back, arms, and shoulders on the floor. Ideally you are trying to touch the floor with your right knee, but the twist is what is important. Hold this position for a slow count of 6, or longer if that is comfortable for you.

(3) Inhale as you return your leg to centre, then lower it. Repeat with the left leg.

BREATHING: Exhale as you go into the pose; inhale when you lower your leg across your body; breathe naturally while you hold the extreme position; inhale as you return to start.

REPETITIONS: Repeat at least twice on each side, alternating.

TIPS: Try to stay relaxed as you do this exercise; pay special attention to your shoulders and the upper part of your back.

Varicose Veins

One in four women and one in ten men suffer from unsightly and sometimes painful varicose veins. This condition often first appears or is made worse by pregnancy, when hormonal changes and pressure caused by the growing fetus can impair circulation in the legs.

A varicose vein is actually a circulatory problem. Ordinarily, the blood that your heart pumps to your lower extremities returns to the upper part of your body through the action of your leg muscles, which squeeze on the veins, in effect pumping the blood upward through a series of one-way valves. When these valves do not function correctly, the blood tends to stay pooled in the lower veins, distending and eventually injuring them.

The most important causes of varicose veins are thought to be inactivity and heredity. You can't do anything about your heredity, but you can make an effort to get plenty of exercise, concentrating on activities that encourage vigorous leg movement, such as walking, running, and bicycling.

Once you have varicose veins, they can't really be cured (except through surgery), but you may be able to keep them from becoming worse and to provide symptomatic relief by putting your feet up whenever you can and avoiding standing or sitting for long periods of time. For example, if you must take a long plane ride, walk up and down the aisle once or twice every hour or so. On long car trips, likewise, stop every hour or so to take a short stroll. While it can help to wear support hose, wearing girdles or crossing your legs can restrict the free return of blood to your heart.

Reverse poses, such as the Half Shoulder Stand described in the section on infertility, are often helpful. Wiggle your toes while you hold one of these poses to increase the muscular pressure on your leg veins.

Haemorrhoids

You may be surprised to learn that haemorrhoids are actually varicose veins of the rectum; like varicose veins of the legs, they are caused partially by heredity and partly by inactivity, particularly sitting a great deal, and they can become much worse during pregnancy, when the pressure of the growing fetus increases congestion in the entire pelvic area. Constipation, too, which is common in pregnancy, can make haemorrhoids worse.

Just as with varicose veins of the legs, the aim in treating and preventing haemorrhoids is to encourage the free return of blood to the heart. All your regular pelvic exercises, particularly the P-C contractions, will help to encourage this return. As with varicose veins of the legs, it's important to walk as much as possible and to avoid sitting or standing for too long in one position.

Any reverse exercise pose will also help. Perform the Half Shoulder Stand as recommended in the section on infertility. While you are holding the pose, rapidly contract your P-C muscle, concentrating on the anal sphincter, 10 times, working up to 20 quick times; this will help to increase the flow of blood throughout the pelvic area.

The following exercise may also help, and as a bonus will help to tighten and tone your derriere:

HIP WALK

POSITION: Sit on the floor, your back straight, your arms held comfortably but not supporting you; your legs are straight out in front of you, your knees slightly bent.

ACTION: Using the muscles of your thighs and buttocks, 'walk' forward, supporting yourself solely on your buttocks and on your feet, which should extend ahead of you as you scoot along the floor. This may seem difficult at first, but you will quickly get the hang of it.

BREATHING: Breathe naturally; do not hold your breath.

REPETITIONS/GOAL: Begin with 5 'steps' on each side, alternating; work up to 10 per side.

The Middle Years: Menopause

Nina, a vivacious and sparkling woman in her forties, has the energy and enthusiasm usually associated with extreme youth. When an acquaintance recently remarked, astonished, 'I didn't know you were forty-nine!' Nina replied, 'I'm not. That's just my age.'

Nina is living proof that growing older does not have to mean growing sicker, less attractive, or less vital. Life, after all, consists of a number of regular, predictable, and perfectly normal body changes. Unfortunately, many women approach these changes with a combination of dread and misunderstanding. Among the most often dreaded and least-understood of these changes is the myth-ridden time known as menopause or change of life. Yet as Nina's example shows, these years can be among the most productive and fulfilling. 'I love it,' she says. 'My children are grown and on their own and for the first time in years I have time for *me*. To tell the truth, I've never felt better or happier.'

Technically, the *menopause* is a one-time event: the actual last period of menstruation, and you can know when that moment has come only a year or two afterwards. The entire process leading to and following the actual menopause is referred to as the climacteric, which literally means a 'rung on a ladder'; popularly, however, 'menopause' refers to the entire process.

Until fairly recently not a great deal was known about this time of life or exactly how it affects women, beyond certain well-understood hormonal changes that result as the ovaries age and begin to slow their production of oestrogen. Although oestrogen production never entirely ceases, except in certain unusual cases, there is usually a period of time during which the body must learn to adjust to a new hormonal balance (other hormones are now acting on the body in *relatively* greater amounts compared to the smaller amount of oestrogen). This hormonal imbalance is known to be responsible for some of the most common symptoms of menopause (although a significant percentage of women never experience *any* clearly defined symptoms). These symptoms may include hot flushes, in which the capillaries near the skin enlarge and fill with blood, causing a feeling of intense heat; profuse perspiration, usually associated with hot flushes; and a loss of elasticity and lubrication in the vagina.

Although many other conditions in older women, ranging from insomnia to osteoporosis (brittle bones) are sometimes associated with the climacteric, there is no evidence that any of these are caused by hormonal imbalance. Many of these occurrences, in fact, are probably the result of the natural process of ageing, combined with lifelong inactivity.

As you approach the climacteric and its aftermath, there are several steps you can take to ensure that it will not be a distressing time for you. Among these are:

1. Learn as much as you can about your body, its anatomy, and its natural changes. A pilot study of menopausal women in New Jersey has discovered that a majority of women in the mid-life do not have even the most rudimentary such knowledge; as a result, they believe such old wives' tales as the myth that menopause causes a woman to lose her sex drive or that she will inevitably become nervous and irritable. The majority of experts now believe that such distressing symptoms are not a natural part of the climacteric at all but are, rather, the result of other factors, such as changing family situations, mid-life career changes, and fear of loss of attractiveness.

The more you learn about the climacteric, the fewer surprises there will be, and the less you will have to fear. The menopausal education programme mentioned earlier is spawning other such groups across the country; in addition, there are a number of excellent books listed in the appendix that can teach you more about your own body and the changes you may expect.

2. Look upon the climacteric as a normal and healthy part of life. After all, your life expectancy is seventy-seven years; therefore, if your menopause occurs between the ages of forty-five and fifty-five (the average), you still have about a third of your life to look forward to. As the authors of *The Ms. Guide to a Woman's Health* put it, the menopause is 'a sign of good health and normal progress through life.'

3. Continue to get plenty of exercise if you have been doing so; if you have not, start an exercise programme with your doctor's advice immediately.

Exercise in the Middle Years

As we have emphasized before, exercise and physical relaxation are extremely important throughout your life; at no other time, though, will exercise make so much of a difference in the *quality* of your life as in the second half. By middle age the natural changes of living, years of inactivity, and the traumas of childbirth have brought many women to a level of reduced health.

This state is *not* inevitable or irreversible, however. In most cases the proper exercises can prevent or alleviate unpleasant symptoms, while a good level of pelvic and cardiovascular fitness will enable you to remain active, attractive, and in good health for many, many years. As a matter of fact, Maria, who is in her fifties, has a stunning figure, with taut skin and firm muscles that would be the envy of a woman of any age. She is living proof that beauty and vitality are not the exclusive property of youth.

Following is an exercise programme for the menopausal and postmenopausal years, with special suggestions for some of the disorders that may (but not necessarily will) develop at this time.

1. Cardiovascular fitness. Although as women we are protected against heart disease to a greater extent than men throughout our lives, this natural protection, thought to be hormonal, *begins to decline with passing years*. After menopause, in fact, the risk rises sharply, although it never becomes so great as for men. For this reason, if you have not done so already, beginning a programme for aerobic fitness is especially important at this time. Not only will such exercise help to improve the health of your heart and circulatory system, it will improve your overall appearance and help to prevent stiff, aching joints.

Women who have never before exercised should check with a doctor, and then, if she or he agrees, begin a simple walking programme. This should be combined with a diet if you are now overweight. For details on aerobics programmes and diet, see the appendix.

173

2. Pelvic fitness. Pelvic fitness exercises for the abdomen, lower back, and P-C are especially important in the middle years, and particularly for women who have had children. Depending on your present condition, you may not wish to progress beyond maintenance on Level I or Level II of this programme; continuing to do your pelvic exercises three times a week (and P-C contractions daily) will help to ensure a good level of continuing pelvic fitness.

3. Learn to relax. A top woman expert on problems of the climacteric states, 'No matter what her physical shape, tension is the number-one problem for a woman at this time of life.' Set aside a certain amount of time every day for one of the relaxation exercises recommended in chapter 14. In addition, taking a yoga or meditation class will greatly increase your ability to cope with stress.

Exercises for Specific Conditions

On the following pages are exercises that can help to relieve or prevent certain conditions that are more prevalent in mid-life. Before you attempt self-treatment for *any* condition, check with a doctor. If you have been told that you must have surgery for a condition such as urinary stress incontinence, ask your doctor's permission to try exercise for a few months first. *This has worked for thousands of women*, and can work for you too if you make up your mind to begin the programme and stick with it!

Pelvic Relaxation

There are a number of conditions that fall under the general term 'pelvic relaxation.' These include 'loose vagina,' which can result in diminished enjoyment of sex for both a woman and her partner; cystocele, in effect a hernia involving a weakness of the bladder wall in which the bladder can press into the vagina; rectocele, a similar weakness in the wall of the rectum; and uterine prolapse, in which a breakdown of all the pelvic ligaments and muscles causes the uterus to actually sag into the vagina, in extreme cases protruding out and between the legs.

A more common complaint, which we have mentioned many times and which often appears in women before menopause, is

174

urinary stress incontinence, in which the part of the P-C that controls the urinary sphincter is so weak that an afflicted woman cannot prevent involuntary leakage of urine when sneezing, laughing, or performing heavy physical activity. Urinary stress incontinence is often associated with the other conditions mentioned above, and it can grow progressively worse. Nora W., a retired teacher in her late fifties, had enjoyed folk dancing her whole life. 'Then I developed this embarrassing problem,' she says. 'I couldn't do any of the fast dances anymore, especially the ones with jumping. It got so bad I quit dancing completely.' Nora's doctor told her surgery was the only answer, but on the advice of friends she tried P-C exercise. 'It was like a miracle,' she says. 'Within five months the condition was gone. Now I'm back to folk dancing—even the heavy Balkan dances.'

Exercises for Urinary Stress Incontinence

If you have symptoms of the conditions mentioned above or a feeling of heaviness and discomfort in the pelvic area, it is essential that you begin doing the P-C contractions recommended for Levels I and II of the Pelvic Fitness Programme. In fact, these exercises are much more important for you than for other women, since your symptoms are evidence that damage has already occurred through childbirth, surgery, or simple inactivity.

In the first part of this book we explained how important it is to do the P-C contractions many times a day. For women with symptoms of pelvic relaxation, frequency is often the key to relief: if it seems like a nuisance, remember that the alternative may be surgery. Even if exercise does not completely clear up the condition, it will help you recover more quickly from any subsequent surgery.

How many contractions should you do? This will depend partly on the present condition of your P-C muscle. For best results, you should do two types of contractions: the fast P-C contractions first described in Level I and the slow, maximum contractions described in Maintenance.

For the fast contractions, your goal is 200 *full* contractions per day. The best way to achieve this goal is to do as many complete, strong contractions at a time as you can. This may be as few as 5 or 6 at first, so you will have to do the exercise many times during the day. However, the condition of your P-C will improve rapidly, and soon you will be able to do many more contractions at a time—so

175

you will have to do them less often. And once you have achieved P-C fitness, you can discontinue the fast contractions and perform the slow contractions on a daily basis for maintenance.

Your goal in the slow contractions is to do 10 full contractions for 6 seconds each. To be effective, the contraction must be held at maximum force for that entire 6 seconds. When you are first starting, do 5 contractions (or as many as you can) for 6 full seconds and gradually build up. When you are able to do 50 fast contractions and 10 full slow contractions for 6 seconds, you can maintain your new level of fitness by performing the slow contractions once a day, when you wake up in the morning. (For complete instructions on P-C contractions, review chapter 8).

Remember that the key to success with this exercise is frequency and persistence. One woman who wanted to avoid surgery for urinary stress incontinence set her kitchen timer to go off every forty-five minutes, reminding her to do her contractions. 'At first it was annoying,' she says. 'I didn't really think it would help, but it did. At the end of six months most of the symptoms were gone. My doctor was as surprised as I was—and nearly as pleased.'

Another woman reports similar results, adding, 'My doctor couldn't believe it. I told him I'd been exercising and he said he wished more of his patients would learn to stick to it. But it wasn't hard—after the first couple of weeks the exercises became automatic.'

Urinary Urgency Incontinence

A condition with similar symptoms but a different cause is urinary urgency incontinence. In this condition the bladder has lost its suppleness and is unable to retain more than small amounts of urine, resulting in frequent, overwhelming impulses to urinate. The P-C is usually too weak to help hold back the flow, so a woman with urgency incontinence finds herself a virtual prisoner, unable to stray far from the vicinity of a toilet.

Urgency incontinence can be overcome by gradually training yourself to wait longer between urinations. For the first week, force yourself to wait ten minutes from the urge to void before actually emptying the bladder. Each week add another ten minutes to the waiting period. Over time this routine will gently stretch the bladder, increasing its capacity. Many women with this condition have managed to increase the time between voidings by up to four hours.

176

In conjunction with the bladder training, perform the P-C contractions recommended in the previous section for better ability to control the flow of urine.

Note: Before beginning this exercise be sure to check with your doctor to make certain that the cause of your urgency incontinence is not a bladder infection or inflammation.

Prolapse

Prolapse of the uterus, perhaps the most extreme of the conditions discussed here, is far less common than it used to be, partly because of improved medical care and partly because women today tend to have fewer children than in the past, resulting in less trauma to the P-C and the pelvic ligaments. Prolapse is usually treated by hysterectomy; in cases where surgery is inadvisable, a pessary, which is a hard rubber ring, is sometimes inserted into the vagina to hold the uterus in place. While prolapse cannot be cured without surgery, it will respond to exercises to strengthen the P-C if the symptoms are not too severe. If you suffer from this condition, in addition to P-C contractions, spend at least one minute a day in a reverse pose, as described in the section on infertility, chapter 17.

Osteoporosis

This is a common condition in which the bones become brittle and lose much of their strength, resulting in easy breaks and, in extreme cases, crippling. Its causes are not completely understood, but it is known to be much more common in women than in men, and particularly in women past menopause. Two important contributors to osteoporosis are lack of calcium and lack of exercise. Make sure that your diet includes plenty of calcium, found in dairy products and leafy green vegetables. In addition, get as much exercise as possible; see the appendix for suggestions on beginning a walking or other aerobic programme.

Back Trouble

'Oh, my aching back.' This familiar refrain is sighed by the majority of Americans at one time or another, particularly by women, who, because of the nature of their lives and the structure of their pelvic area, seem more prone to back stress than men are.

Lorraine, a fashion industry executive in her mid-forties, is a case in point. Although very conscious of her appearance, dieted to razor-slimness and a devotee of 'flab-reducing massages' at a health spa, Lorraine has been plagued for years by severe, debilitating pains in her lower back. Several doctors have recommended that she do exercises to strengthen the muscles in her abdomen and provide flexibility in her lower back but, 'Somehow I just can't do it,' she says. Instead, she has spent a fortune on pain-killers, tranquillizers, and doctors, ranging from chiropractors to neurosurgeons to psychiatrists.

Lorraine's reluctance to exercise for her back pain is probably due to the fact that it seems too easy a solution. Our answer to that is a simple one: why not give it a try? The fact is that the number-one cause of back pain is lack of exercise; it only makes sense that exercise should be an important part of the treatment.

The reasons so many women begin to suffer back pain in their middle years are many: important among them are years of poor posture and inactivity combined with back stress during pregnancy and while raising small children. The result is a lower back that curves abnormally, placing stress on the muscles and ligaments of the pelvic area. This problem is usually made worse by flabby abdominal muscles, which are unable to keep the spine and pelvis in proper alignment.

Because of the vulnerability of the joint that unites the pelvis with the last lumbar (lower back) vertebra, where most forward and backward movement of the body takes place, it is here that most serious problems occur, including 'slipped disks.' (This misnomer refers to a condition that is medically called 'herniated disk,' and which is actually a rupture of the outer covering of the cushionlike disks that separate the vertebrae.)

Even if you never suffer a slipped disk, poor muscular alignment in the lower back can still cause problems ranging from a nagging, aching feeling to the sometimes severe pain of sciatica, and other disk trouble.

If poor muscle tone were the only culprit in back pain, simply doing the pelvic fitness exercises would help you to achieve and then maintain the strength you need to prevent problems in the lower back. While the programme is helpful, however, pelvic alignment is more than a matter of muscular strength. The fact is, poor posture develops in much the same way as the lines on your face: your daily habits, good and bad; the nature of your work and your leisure

178

activities; even the shoes you wear all go into creating your habitual posture. For most of us, unfortunately, these daily activities involve desks and counters that are the wrong height, inefficient carrying and lifting, and high-heeled shoes that throw our bodies out of alignment.

Thus, for many of us the pelvis itself is not placed where it should be; the resulting muscular stresses can be a prime contributor to backaches and even injury. Happily, the bad habits we have learned can be readily unlearned, and in a very simple way, by consciously moving your pelvis into proper alignment until that alignment becomes natural.

The following two exercises take only a few seconds and can help relieve any stress in your lower back, as well as help you to learn how it feels to hold your pelvic area correctly. Perform one or both of them twice a day and as many other times as you think of it for improved appearance, decreased fatigue, and freedom from an aching back.

PELVIC PRESS I

PURPOSE: To realign your pelvis and help you learn how it feels to have your back in proper alignment.
POSITION: Lie on your back, your knees bent, your feet flat on the floor close to your buttocks.
ACTION: Raise your pelvic area, 'tucking' it under while at the same time pressing your lower back flat against the floor and tightening your stomach muscles. Hold for a count of 4, then relax and repeat.
BREATHING: Breathe naturally; do not hold your breath.
REPETITIONS: Do 2 of these, twice or more often every day.
TIPS: As you perform this exercise, keep your shoulders and upper body relaxed.

PELVIC PRESS II

PURPOSE: To realign your pelvis and help you learn how it feels to have correct posture while you are standing.
POSITION: Stand with your back against a wall, your feet about 6 inches from the wall and comfortably apart.
ACTION: Pressing your lower back into the wall, slowly move your heels to the wall until they are about 2 inches away. At this point you should be in contact with the wall at the heels, buttocks, lower back,

and shoulders. Contract your abdominal and buttocks muscles and hold for a count of 4. Release and return to start.

BREATHING: Breathe naturally; do not hold your breath.

REPETITIONS: Do this twice each time you do it. The more often during the day you practise it, the more natural this position will become, and the less stress you will feel.

TIPS: Remember to keep your neck and shoulders relaxed as you perform this exercise.

To maintain good posture, consciously keep your pelvis 'tucked' when walking and standing. Standing or sitting for long periods of time can cause tension in the lower back—whenever you must work in one position, take frequent breaks and walk around or practise Pelvic Press I or II.

Simply becoming conscious of your poor postural habits can make a big difference. As one exercise student puts it, 'For the first time I'm learning what it feels like *not* to have a backache.'

Dowager's Hump

This is another fairly common condition that usually does not appear until old age but begins much earlier. It can result in a hunched, bent-over posture with a 'hump' of fatty tissue at the back of the neck.

As with most back trouble, the principal causes of dowager's hump are muscular imbalance and inactivity; the upper back muscles, which are already weak in most women, become stretched and pulled forward by the much stronger (relatively) front muscles, which receive more exercise in the course of daily living. Osteoporosis contributes to and complicates the resulting abnormal curve. Once you have developed this condition, not much can be done to cure it, but your appearance can be improved with exercise. It is important for younger women to begin to strengthen the upper back and to stretch the chest muscles to help prevent this unsightly condition. The following exercises are not only good for preventing dowager's hump, they will increase upper-body flexibility in women of any age.

SPINE STRAIGHTENER

POSITION: Lie on your back, both knees bent, your knees and feet together, your heels as close to your buttocks as possible. Your tailbone should be raised slightly off the floor, your whole spine flat against the floor, especially in the lower back area (check with a finger if necessary). Place your arms straight out to the sides, your palms up and your thumbs on the floor, your neck pressed against the floor.

ACTION: Keeping your arms straight and your elbows and thumbs in contact with the floor, slowly slide your arms along the floor toward your head. As you do so, be sure to keep your lower back on the floor. Move your arms in an arc as high as you can, then hold this position for a count of 8, and slowly return to starting position.

BREATHING: Breathe naturally; do not hold your breath.

REPETITIONS/GOAL: Begin with 4; work up to 8.

TIPS: The effect of this exercise will be lost if you are not in contact with the floor at all times at these three points: lower back, thumbs, and elbows. If you can do the exercise easily with no sense of strain, you probably do not need it. If it is difficult or if you feel a pulling in the backs of your arms and the upper back, continue to practise.

SPINE STRETCHER

POSITION: Lie on your stomach, your chin resting on the floor, your arms outstretched on the floor in front of you, close to your head (they should touch your ears).

ACTION: Keeping your head relaxed, lift your right arm as high as you can in the air. Do not twist your body and do not move your neck. Hold a moment, then lower, and repeat with the other arm.

BREATHING: Inhale as you lift your arm, exhale when you lower it. Perform this exercise in a rhythm with your normal breathing patterns.

REPETITIONS: 8 times with each arm, alternating.

TIPS: This exercise is good for releasing tension from the upper back area. If you can't lift your arms very high at first, just continue doing the exercise and you will soon see improvement.

STANDING SPINE STRETCH

NOTE: This exercise can be performed by women of any age. It relaxes the upper back and improves posture.

POSITION: Stand comfortably with your back close to a wall, your feet comfortably apart, your heels approximately 2 inches from the wall.

ACTION: Slightly bend your knees, pushing your whole spine against the wall, making certain the lower back is in contact with the wall. Holding your back against the wall, slowly slide both your arms up over your head, keeping your back, thumbs, and elbows in contact with the wall (this will resemble the Spine Straightener). Go only as far as you can without straining, then return to start.

BREATHING: Breathe naturally; don't hold your breath.

REPETITIONS/GOAL: 4 times at first; work up to 8.

The Later Years

A statistic that may surprise you is that the fastest-growing segment of our population is women over the age of sixty-five. Within fifty years, in fact, older women are expected to outnumber older men by eleven million.

Although older women are a neglected minority today, in the near future all segments of society will increasingly cater to their needs and wants. Thus, if we are in good health, we can look forward to long years in which we are important and respected participants in the life around us.

The biggest obstacle to realization of that dream is one of attitude —the attitude that old age must be a time of decrepitude. Tens of thousands of older Americans know that this view is not correct; still, many of us, and particularly women, expect to gradually become more and more feeble as we grow older.

Stevia Chaffee was one of those who believed this common myth. In her mid-fifties she developed asthma and consequently stopped her lifelong practice of exercise. It was only when her daughter, Suzy, the famous Olympic skier, literally forced her to start working out again that Stevia regained her youthful health and vigour. A very young-looking sixty-seven, Stevia today does yoga, gymnastics, daily walking, and any other activity that seems interesting to her. 'People are astonished when they see how fit I am,' she relates. 'In fact, in one advanced exercise class I was able to do splits when none of the younger women could. All older women should learn what exercise can do for them.'

Stevia's enthusiasm is echoed by a seventy-year-old member of one of Maria's fitness classes, who credits continuing pelvic exercises with her flexibility and good sex life.

The most important advice we can give you in regard to your own age is to keep moving. You will not find yourself confined to a wheelchair if you keep your body supple and your joints limber. If you can, join an exercise class for older people (check with your local YWCA for information). If you do not have access to such a programme or prefer to work out on your own, try the following programme.

1. Walk. For details about creating your own walking programme, see the appendix.

2. Perform the Pelvic Fitness Programme at Level I three or more times a week. Do P-C contractions daily to keep your pelvic floor supple and strong and to prevent symptoms of pelvic relaxation.

3. Do 'belly breathing,' as described in chapter 14. Decreased lung capacity, shallow breathing, and consequent fatigue are common problems in older women; taking two to three complete deep breaths at least three times a day will help to expand your chest and increase your vitality.

4. Do exercises for flexibility of your whole body at least three times a week. For most older women, the demands of a growing family and a busy career no longer provide an excuse not to exercise. Setting aside as few as ten minutes a day will cause a marked improvement in the entire quality of your life, the way you look, and the way you feel. You can alternate the following exercises with your regular Pelvic Fitness workout.

Upper Back Exercises

To prevent or control dowager's hump, as well as to relieve tension in the neck and upper back, do one or more of the exercises for the upper back recommended in the previous chapter.

Warm-ups

Perform as many of the warm-ups from chapter 7 as you can comfortably manage. If you can go through the entire series (which takes only a few minutes) it will greatly increase the flexibility of your whole body. In any case, be sure to do the Shrug, Exercise 2.

184

BICYCLE

POSITION: Lie on your back, both legs bent, your entire spine flat against the floor (if necessary, check with a finger at the small of the back). Your hands should be at your sides and your whole body relaxed.

ACTION: (1) Slowly extend your right leg, pushing your heel against the floor, until the leg is straight.

(2) With a continuous movement, raise the right leg toward the ceiling as far as you can, keeping it straight.

(3) Bend the leg and pull it in (toward your chest); return to start and rest for a few moments, then repeat with the other leg.

BREATHING: Breathe naturally; do not hold your breath.

REPETITIONS: 4 times with each leg, alternating.

TIPS: If this exercise is easy for you, or when it becomes easy, you can increase the stretch throughout your entire back and lower leg by pointing your heel toward the ceiling as you raise your leg.

LEG OVER

POSITION: Lie on your back, your legs straight, your arms stretched out along the floor at shoulder level.

ACTION: (1) Slowly lift your right leg toward the ceiling, keeping your lower back on the floor (don't arch it).

(2) When the leg is as high as it will go comfortably, lower it across your body toward your left hand. The *aim* is to touch your left hand with your right foot. If you can only barely cross the other leg, that is fine to begin with. Return to start and repeat with the other leg.

BREATHING: Breathe naturally; don't hold your breath.

REPETITIONS/GOAL: Start with 2 for each leg, alternating; build to 4.

TIPS: The point of this exercise is to get the stretch. Go only as far as your body will comfortably permit, without forcing. Gradually you will become more limber.

SITTING TWIST

POSITION: Sit comfortably on a stool, your right knee crossed over the left, your left hand on top of your right knee. Your right arm is bent, with your right hand lightly resting on the small of your back toward the side.

ACTION: Inhale, and as you do so, turn your upper torso to the right as far as you can. Try to lead with your shoulder, turning your head and pointing your right elbow straight behind. Turn as far as you can, as if trying to see someone standing behind you. Hold for a count of 2 in the extreme position, then inhale and return to start. Repeat on the other side, with your left knee crossed over your right.

BREATHING: Inhale as you twist and as you return to start; at other times breathe naturally.

REPETITIONS: 2 on each side, alternating.

TIPS: Don't strain in this position, but do try to develop the greatest twist that you can.

FORWARD BEND

POSITION: Sit on the floor, your legs straight in front of you, your hands at your sides.

ACTION: (1) Inhale, lifting both arms over your head, then exhale, lowering your arms and head toward your knees, your back straight. Hold this position a few seconds, then

(2) Inhaling, slide your hands along the tops of your legs until you return to the upright position.

(3) Clasp your hands behind you and lean back, keeping your head high and raising your straight arms (hands still clasped) out behind you as high as you can. Hold for a count of 4, lower your arms, and relax.

BREATHING: Except where noted, breathe naturally.

REPETITIONS: 4 times.

TIP: If you feel a sense of strain in your lower back during any part of this exercise, bend your knees slightly. If you still feel a strain, try doing it in a chair. Very old people are able to do this and receive the benefits.

STANDING STRETCH

POSITION: Stand comfortably, your legs a few inches apart.

ACTION: (1) Lift both arms straight up toward the ceiling. Now stretch your right hand, palm up, upward as far as you can reach. In a fluid motion repeat the stretch with the left hand, then with both together.

186

(2) Slowly push both arms as far as you can toward the back, keeping them straight. Inhale and slowly make half circles in the air with both hands as you return them to the sides of your body.

BREATHING: Inhale as you stretch, exhale as you lower your arms.

REPETITIONS: Do the complete motion 2 times.

TIPS: Perform this exercise very slowly and without straining. Try to feel the stretch throughout your entire body.

The Sexual Woman

A prominent exercise authority claims that sexual intercourse burns '200 calories per couple per incident.' Whether or not that is true, there is no doubt that sex is as vital to well-being as food, sleep, and exercise. In fact, you can think of sex as a kind of physical and emotional health regimen. In *Our Bodies, Ourselves* and other women's health books, intercourse itself is cited as a good toning exercise for the muscles of the pelvic floor. And Masters and Johnson point out that continuing to engage in sexual activity through menopause and beyond helps to avoid sexual problems in old age.

To achieve optimal lifelong sexual functioning, two things are required: an acceptance of sex as a natural, healthy part of life and a good degree of pelvic fitness.

The importance of a strong P-C muscle in sexual enjoyment is seldom discussed in our culture, probably because of lingering attitudes that women are not interested in sex or that such things are unmentionable. Yet in some other societies, P-C contractions are routinely taught to marriageable young women. According to the authors of *Woman's Orgasm*, there is an African tribe in which good P-C control is a *prerequisite* to marriage. A medieval Indian text, the *Anagaranga*, contains a passage in which young women are urged to spend long hours in practice until they have complete control of their vaginal muscles.

Of course, these exercises were recommended primarily for the sake of the man's sexual pleasure, but the truth is that a strong P-C muscle improves sexual functioning and greatly increases sexual pleasure for the woman as well. In fact, a firm and strong P-C muscle is *essential* for optimal sexual response.

This is so for a variety of reasons. Among the most obvious is that a firm, snug vagina increases friction during sexual intercourse. Just

189

as important, a strong P-C allows for increased sexual sensations within the entire pelvic area. Dr. J. P. Greenhill, who has treated countless women for urinary stress incontinence and other symptoms of pelvic relaxation, reports that because the P-C is generously supplied with nerves that respond to touch and pressure, exercises to strengthen this muscle activate those nerves, enhancing 'sexual sensory perception.' He tells of women who, having lost their enjoyment of sex following difficult childbirth, found that exercise alone helped them to regain their former level of sexual response.

Furthermore, the knowledge that one is in good physical condition can be important psychologically. A woman who had visited Maria's infertility classes reported that both her and her husband's enjoyment of sex had greatly increased as a direct result of the exercises she had done for her overall fitness and especially for the strength of the P-C muscle. 'I knew from the exercises that I was a good lover,' she says. 'When I didn't have to worry about whether or not I was pleasing my husband, I felt freer to enjoy myself.'

Even women who have never had doubts about or difficulties with sex report good results from P-C exercises. 'It was always good and now it's better,' is a common response. Or, as a young teacher put it, 'Sex is more exciting to me now. I have a feeling of power. Maybe I shouldn't say this, but it's great to see how much control you can have over your partner.'

* * *

On the following pages are exercises designed to enhance your own and your partner's enjoyment of sex. This is *not* a sexual therapy programme: if you have problems with painful intercourse, or lack of feeling, by all means speak frankly to your doctor to make sure there's no hidden physical difficulty—several gynaecological conditions can contribute to painful or unpleasurable intercourse.

Exercises for Better Sex

1. Aerobic fitness. Although it is true that almost anyone, no matter what her physical condition, can *have* sex, to be a fully functioning, enjoying sexual being, it is necessary to be as physically fit as possible. In a survey of married joggers, writer Valerie Andrews found that nearly all reported that their sex lives had improved since

they began running. 'Most of them said they weren't having sex in greater quantity, but that the *quality* had improved,' she reports. 'The women especially said that they got more out of sex because they weren't tired all the time.'

For information on beginning an aerobic fitness programme, see the appendix.

2. P-C Fitness. Of all the muscles in your body, your P-C is the most important for optimal sexual functioning (next most important are your other pelvic muscles—those of the abdomen and lower back). To gain maximum control of your P-C and thus to ensure maximum sensory enjoyment, practise all P-C exercises in the Pelvic Fitness Programme until you can do them easily.

The best exercise for sexual feeling is the P-C Isolation as performed on Level III (Pelvic Floor Exercise 2). If you have ever had a problem with lack of sexual feeling or with inhibition, this exercise can be especially helpful for you. As you do it, concentrate on the actual sensations that your pelvic contractions produce. Learning to recognize and enjoy these feelings will greatly add to your enjoyment of sex.

With your partner's cooperation, you can also practice P-C contractions while having sex—in fact, strong voluntary P-C contractions during sex are one of the goals of this programme. If you feel comfortable about it, ask your partner for feedback on the strength of your contractions.

3. Relaxation. Knowing how to relax your muscles selectively is an important part of good sex. One reason for this is that, psychologically, women tend to be more easily distracted from their own sexual feelings than men are. If your buttocks and your abdomen are tense while you make love, they can block off the sexual sensations in the rest of your body. To learn to perceive sexual feelings in your pelvis while consciously relaxing, practice Differential Relaxation (chapter 14), concentrating on the part of the exercise in which you contract the P-C while keeping all other parts of your body totally relaxed.

4. Flexibility and control. The following exercises concentrate for the most part on achieving free movement of pelvis. The majority of women have a very rigid pelvis, which can undermine health and sexual functioning by causing aches and pains as well as discomfort

191

in certain positions during sex. Conversely, the more flexible your pelvic area, the more effortless and enjoyable sex will be for you.

PELVIC LOOSENER

PURPOSE: To free your pelvis from tension and allow complete and full movement of the entire pelvic area.

POSITION: Stand with your feet comfortably apart, your knees slightly bent. Be sure that you are comfortable, because during the performance of this exercise your legs and upper torso should not move.

ACTION: (1) Inhale, and gently tilt your pelvis (as if to spill water out of the pelvic 'bowl' to the front), pushing your tailbone back and upward.

(2) Exhale, gently swinging your pelvis in the opposite direction (as if to spill water from the *back* of the pelvic 'bowl'). Imagine that you are trying to see your pubic bone, while not moving your legs or upper body. Repeat (1) and continue, alternating in a gentle, swinging motion.

These actions may be somewhat difficult at first, particularly if your pelvic area is stiff. If you find that your pelvis will not move freely, or does not move much, don't get discouraged—just keep practising. When you have mastered the gentle back and front swinging of your pelvis, add

(3) Twist your upper body to the right and repeat the movements in (1) and (2) above. The front and backward pelvic swing will now be performed diagonally with respect to your legs.

(4) Twist your upper body to the left and repeat.

BREATHING: See instructions above. The entire movement should be gentle and unrushed, in a rhythm with your natural breathing.

REPETITIONS/GOALS: Parts (1) and (2), 8 times each. Parts (3) and (4), 4 complete swings on each side, alternating.

TIPS: Remember to keep your upper body and legs motionless; check your shoulders to be sure they are relaxed.

PELVIC RAISE

PURPOSE: To further increase the flexibility of your pelvic area and to aid in relaxation of all the pelvic muscles.

POSITION: Lie on your stomach, your legs together, your head resting comfortably on your arms.

ACTION: Keeping your whole body on the floor, lift your pelvis upward. Stick your buttocks up in the air, imagining that a string is attached to your tailbone and that the string is pulling you up toward the ceiling. You may slightly bend your knees as your tailbone rises, but keep the rest of your body totally relaxed. Hold for a slow count of 8, then relax.

BREATHING: Breathe naturally; don't hold your breath.

REPETITIONS: 4 times.

FROG

PURPOSE: To tone and relieve tension in the genital area.

POSITION: Kneel down, your knees as wide apart as possible, your toes touching in the back. Your buttocks should be resting on your heels, your torso straight, and your hands on top of your knees.

ACTION: Remaining in this position, take 6 complete belly breaths (chapter 14).

TIPS: Although it seems deceptively easy, this is an advanced exercise and should be attempted only after you have achieved some degree of flexibility of the pelvic area. As you continue to practise it, try to increase the distance between your knees.

THIGH TWIST

PURPOSE: To promote flexibility of the entire pelvic area and to allow the pelvic organs to move into their natural positions. This exercise is also excellent for stretching the lower back and backs of the thighs.

POSITION: Sit in tailor fashion (with your legs crossed in front of you).

ACTION: (1) Pull the right leg over the left knee, bringing your right heel as close as possible to your left thigh, and the left heel as close as possible to your right thigh (use your hands for assistance, if necessary). Your right knee should be directly on top of your left knee, or as close to this as possible. Breathing normally, hold for a slow count of 10.

(2) Repeat, with your left knee over the right one.

REPETITIONS: 2 on each side, alternating.

Exercise and Orgasm

It used to be thought that any woman who had difficulty achieving orgasm, especially during sexual intercourse, was suffering from a form of psychological 'frigidity.' Depending on the myth you subscribed (or subscribe) to, the cause of this might be an unresolved Electra complex, fear of domination by men, or inability to accept one's role as a woman.

This attitude has changed drastically in recent years, largely due to the work of Masters and Johnson, who showed that orgasm occurs in response to a buildup of muscular and nervous tension in the pelvic area, with the sensation concentrated in the clitoris, and that orgasm itself is a release of that tension, accompanied by strong contractions of the pelvic muscles.

Thus, the modern view is that for the majority of women, difficulty in achieving orgasm is largely the result of insufficient stimulation of the clitoris. The causes of this might include lack of knowledge or interest on the part of a sexual partner and shyness or lack of knowledge on the part of the nonorgasmic woman. Another important cause of orgasmic problems, however, is poor pelvic fitness.

All this is not to say that psychological factors are not important in orgasmic capability—attitude and background are essential factors in all forms of sexual expression. But just as important—and in some cases most important—is the strength and control of the P-C muscle.

'I remember the first time I heard about sex in relation to muscular control,' says Caryl, a member of a postexercise discussion group. 'I was involved with a man for the first time and I asked a girlfriend if she had orgasms. She told me she always did, from the very first time she had made love. I couldn't believe it, because I never had them. She said, "It's easy. You just squeeze this muscle that's up inside you." I thanked her for the advice, but I remember thinking, "What muscle? I don't have a muscle there." '

Caryl's confusion is typical of the many women who have never realized that they do in fact have a vaginal muscle that they can control. That muscle is, of course, the P-C, and while P-C strength can't *guarantee* more and better orgasms, an improved sex life is one of the benefits most often mentioned by women who do exercises for the pelvic floor.

If you have ever had difficulty in achieving orgasms, we recommend that, in addition to performing exercises for pelvic fitness, you also become as informed as possible about your body and its sexual responses. Confusion about your own sexuality is nothing to be ashamed of; in the *Hite Report* a large number of women admitted that they were not sure whether or not they had ever had orgasms. Since the female orgasm—unlike the male orgasm, which is unmistakable—is now known to vary tremendously, it is no wonder that many women are confused and worried about whether they are living up to some ideal image. Not only do normal orgasms vary from intense, multiple 'peak experiences' to a series of gentle, peaceful contractions, orgasms may be experienced differently by the same woman at different times.

In the appendix, we list a number of books that will help you to learn more about your own sexual responses, as well as a book offering a step-by-step programme for learning to achieve orgasms.

Whether or not you have difficulty in achieving orgasms, the exercises in the Pelvic Fitness Programme are almost certain to increase the sensations you feel during sex. If you now have orgasms easily, they will probably become more intense and frequent. If you have orgasms occasionally, or with difficulty, they will probably become easier and more frequent.

Women who never have orgasms or have them only rarely should be especially conscientious about performing all exercises in the Pelvic Fitness Programme, especially the P-C Isolation. As we explained earlier, this exercise will not only strengthen your pelvic floor, it will teach you what the sensations arising here feel like. It's entirely possible that you, like many women, have simply not learned to recognize these responses or have unconsciously blocked them out of your life.

Linda G., a young married woman who began doing pelvic exercises for infertility problems, explained that while she never had difficulty achieving orgasm, after she began the exercises, 'They became more intense—I think it wasn't so much that the muscles were stronger but that I was really *aware* of them for the first time.'

It is our hope that pelvic fitness will make your sex life richer and more enjoyable. However, we urge you to remember that orgasm is only one aspect of sex, and not necessarily the most important one; that sexual pleasure is a process, rather than a goal; and finally, that physical and emotional communication with your partner are the hallmarks of a healthy and loving sex life.

How to Begin an Aerobics Programme

Aerobic exercise, which strengthens your heart, lungs, and circulatory system, is the only way to achieve overall physical fitness. Although you can get aerobic exercise in a variety of ways, including running, swimming, jumping rope, cycling, and some other activities, walking and jogging are probably the most practical exercises for most women. They require the least time for benefits, they require no special equipment or previous experience, and they can be done by women of any age starting from almost any level of physical condition.

Following are suggestions for beginning an aerobic walking programme. If you find this programme too easy, or are already reasonably fit, try a more strenuous regimen, such as jogging or swimming. For information on other aerobics programmes, see the bibliography.

1. Get a checkup and tell your doctor what you are planning to do. Medical evaluation is especially important for women over thirty-five, those who have not exercised in a year or more, and anyone who is overweight. If you have a heart condition or circulatory problems, you should begin an aerobics programme *only under medical supervision*. Many YMCAs offer supervised cardiac rehabilitation programmes.

2. Get a good pair of shoes. The type of running shoes known as 'training shoes' are best because they support your whole foot and absorb shock. Do *not* try aerobic walking in high heels.

3. Walk *continuously* and *briskly*. In order to receive aerobic benefits you must exert yourself enough to raise your pulse above 120 beats

per minute. Your breathing should be fast, but not so heavy that you cannot talk, and you should walk briskly enough to break out in a sweat. Walking slowly down the street and window-shopping will not give you aerobic benefits, nor will walking on crowded sidewalks where you must frequently pause for traffic lights. The best places to do aerobic walking are parks and high school or college tracks.

4. Begin at a pace that is comfortable for you and work up gradually. Your goal is to cover each mile in 20 minutes or faster.

5. Schedule: The first week walk continuously for 20 minutes, 5 times a week. If this is too difficult for you, begin with as many minutes of brisk walking as you can without becoming extremely short of breath. If 20 minutes of walking is easy for you, begin with 25 or even 30 minutes. When you can easily walk 20 minutes at a brisk pace, add 5 minutes of walking per workout each week.

Your goal is to walk briskly for 30 to 45 minutes, 4 to 5 times a week. The *minimum* is thus 30 minutes, 4 times a week. This schedule will provide a good level of aerobic fitness; for even greater fitness increase the amount of time that you spend walking, or move into a more strenuous programme such as jogging or swimming.

How Aerobics Can Help You Lose Weight

Fitness experts agree that people who combine diet with vigorous exercise tend to lose faster. Aerobic exercises are best for this purpose because they burn a significant number of calories. For example, walking or running 1 mile burns approximately 100 calories. If you walk at a 20-minute pace for half an hour, 5 times a week (total 7½ miles), you are burning around 750 calories per week. Since one pound is 'worth' approximately 3, 500 calories, this will result in a steady weight loss of roughly a pound a month. This may not sound like much, but if you *combine* that walking programme with a moderate diet, eliminating, say, 200 calories per day from your food intake, the combined calorie deficit quickly adds up.

Furthermore, you will begin to look slimmer even before weight loss shows up on the scale because you will be building muscle tissue, which weighs more than fat but takes up less space. Research indicates that when diet is combined with exercise the weight lost is mostly fat and water, while if you remain sedentary you will also lose muscle. There is also evidence that exercise helps to decrease the 'transit time' of food within your digestive system, so that fewer calories may be absorbed. Finally, as any very active person will confirm, regular vigorous exercise actually diminishes appetite, helping you to respond to hunger signals rather than to external cues such as the sight of food.

Mechanical Aids for Exercising the P-C Muscle

Some women, because of psychological resistance or severe damage to the P-C, are unable to do P-C contractions as we recommend them in this book. For such women, there are mechanical aids available. These devices are not easy to obtain, and are best used under the supervision of a doctor. If you feel you want to use such an aid, be frank with your doctor, perhaps showing her or him this book.

There are other devices on the market that purport to help in strengthening the P-C muscle, but it is doubtful they will do any good. There is one device that we know to be helpful in strengthening the P-C.

Perineometer

This device, invented by Dr. Arnold Kegel, is used to measure the strength of P-C contractions. Since it clearly indicates the strength of each contraction, it can be used as a biofeedback device. This can be especially helpful for women with extremely poor P-C tone—the gauge on the perineometer will show progress, no matter how minuscule, and no matter how difficult it is for the woman to sense her own contractions.

At present perineometers are very difficult to obtain in the U.K. but can be bought in the U.S.A.

Index